How To Develop Boys To Men

How To Develop Boys To Men

**For The Prevention of
The Narcissistic Personality Disorder**

Willie B. Williams II, M.A., LPC

Hardcover ISBN: 979-8-8229-2525-0
Paperback ISBN: 979-8-8229-2526-7

PALMETTO
PUBLISHING
Charleston, SC
www.PalmettoPublishing.com

Special Dedication

This book is prayerfully dedicated to
all our Wonderful Grandchildren and Beautiful Girls
Alaina, Olivia, and Flora III

It is specifically dedicated to the Boys that
are on their way to ManTown the City of Gold
Tre'- Will – JC - Bishop

Contents

Acknowledgments

I truly want to thank my wife Flora for her unwavering support. I would also like to acknowledge the numerous contributions that I have received from my team. My team, who just happens to be my children from oldest to youngest Genesis, Elizabeth, Willie and Flora II and our wonderful Son-In-Law CJ. All the women, men, boys and girls I have counseled over the past 40 years who have inspired me to write this book. In memory of our parents who without them this book would not be possible. Of course, all the thanks and glory goes to God for without him I could do nothing. I believe he has given me the assignment to help others in building strong and healthy families.

 # Foreword

One of the greatest challenges facing our nation today is the lack of loving, caring, and responsible fathers in the home - men who can lead, protect, and provide for their families. This has created a void (physically, emotionally, and spiritually) in the lives of countless children and has had a devastating impact on families.

For many decades, our culture has devalued the role of fathers and redefined what it means to be a man. Many young boys and adolescents, in turn, have looked elsewhere for role models. In the absence of strong and consistent guidance, they often turn to things that seemingly bring satisfaction, but in reality cause harm to themselves and others. Young boys, especially, fall prey to the lies they are told regarding what it takes to be a man. They become self-centered, failing to consider how their actions impact those around them. They engage in risky and destructive behaviors that prevent them from reaching their God-given potential. In the end, they grow physically, but fail to become the men that are so desperately needed in our world today.

In "How to Develop Boys to Men," Willie B. Williams offers solutions to a great challenge confronting our society and presents readers with principles to live by, that if implemented, will change lives for the better. Having faced the challenge himself during his early years growing up in the Fifth Ward of Houston, Texas, Mr. Williams speaks from experience. He recognized even at a young age something was amiss in his life and that children should not be left to fend for themselves without the leadership and direction of a responsible father. Mr. Williams made a commitment to himself that when he became a father he would always be there for his children. He stayed true to that commitment and, in his search for something greater, found the city of "MANTOWN" where men "walk the streets ... dressed from head to toe in wisdom and maturity." Mr. Williams became a man of great character; a wise and godly man who loves his wife, children, and grandchildren. His wife of over 45 years loves and respects him for who he is, and his children are eternally grateful to him for the foundation he laid for them growing up. By every measure, Mr. Williams has been a success in life. He has excelled personally and professionally. God has richly blessed him. The principles that Mr. Williams learned and lived by are principles that he wants every young boy to learn so that they, too, can find "MANTOWN" and be the kind of men that their families need to successfully navigate this life and find meaning, purpose, and hope.

I encourage you to read this book from a man that I consider a dear and trusted friend - one whom I love and respect for his wisdom, knowledge, and manner of life. As you read and study the material found within these pages, put aside "Little Boy Thinking," and stand on the principles that Mr. Williams so clearly articulates. You will reap the benefits in your own life and become a great blessing to future generations as they learn from your example what it means to be a "MANTOWN" man.

Stephen D. Green, Ph.D.

Introduction

ManTown – City of Gold

Some people do not believe that a place exists where real men roam the countryside, receiving the respect and honor they have earned. They say it is all a myth that such a people and a place exist. But do not believe or accept their cynical doubt. Do not buy into the skepticism. There is a MANTOWN! Some have called it the City of Gold.

Outside the gates of MANTOWN these men have left their little boy ways. They walk the streets dressed from head to toe in wisdom and maturity. They are proud and daring yet calm and controlled. It is a place where fathers are viewed by their children as heroes, strong men, providers, and protectors. Their spouses see them as worthy of respect and fitted for love. They are all men in the superlative degree.

Little boys come into this world searching year after year for MANTOWN, the City of Gold., But so few have found it that many have come to think this town is only a legend. It is my hope that the information found in this book will help some boys make it to the land they seek. This book can be used as a map for the journey.

To make this journey you will not drive a car, ride a bus, or board a plane. If you climb aboard this MANTOWN message, you will travel miles without taking a step.

In fact, that is the secret of MANTOWN; the miles you travel are mental. Your travel does not consist of physical steps but mental concepts.

There is only one way to live in MANTOWN and that is for MANTOWN to live in you. You will know that you're living in MANTOWN when your life and your love and your deeds are true.

Who Am I and Why Do I
Write About "ManTown"?

I am Willie B. Williams Jr. I was born in the Fifth Ward of Houston, Texas. When I was growing up, they called my neighborhood the "Bloody Fifth". It was a rough, tough neighborhood. I am one of nine children. I was right in the middle with two older brothers and two younger brothers, two older sisters and two younger sisters. The first six or seven years of my life my father struggled with gambling. During that time, he wasn't around much. Needless to say, our need was great, and the money was low. I am proud to say that after he was converted to Christ, he did his best to turn his life around and serve God.

However, those early years were hard on me. Fear and poverty were no strangers to my family during those years. In our neighborhood one of our toys was the flat tires left on the side of the road or in a field. I remember, at about six years old, rolling my tire down the sidewalk. I suddenly pulled my tire over to an old white abandoned house with the paint peeling off it. I was by myself. I was feeling scared, lonely, and hungry. I said to myself, "Something is wrong with this. I shouldn't have to go through this all by myself. Somebody is supposed to be here with me." That's when it happened! That's when I said something to myself that would shape my future and change the trajectory of my life. I said, "When I get children, I'm not going to leave them out here by themselves." I said, "When I get children, I'm going to be there for my children."

Because I had a little speed you could say I ran out of a bad situation. What I mean is I received a track scholarship to attend college. I received an AA degree from Southwestern Christian College in Terrell Texas, a B.A. degree in Bible and Political Science at Harding University in Searcy Arkansas, and a master's degree in religion and psychology at Harding Graduate School in Memphis, Tennessee. I completed Post Graduate hours at The University of Arkansas and Texas A&M University to secure the necessary hours to be a Licensed Professional Counselor. I earned a Lifetime Teacher's Certification and worked in the classroom and district office of the Houston Independent School District for over ten years. I was the Director of Counseling and a College Professor at Southwestern Christian College, a College Therapist at Blinn College in Brenham, Texas, and a Therapist at A&M Christian Counseling Center in Bryan, Texas.

I have been in the ministry for over forty years. I am the author of two books, "Seven Steps To Parenting Power" and "Mama Is That A Man". As a singer and song writer, I have written and produced seven albums and CD's. My latest release is entitled "Show Me A Man; The MANTOWN Project."

But of all the things that I have been blessed to accomplish, one thing stands out above the rest. I am most grateful for the family God has allowed me to enjoy. God allowed me to keep a promise I made to myself at six years old. I have been blessed to be the husband of Flora Williams for over forty-five years. We were blessed with four wonderful children. I saw all four come from their mother's womb. I was there for them when they went to their first kindergarten class. I was their first coach. All four graduated from high school and college and I was in the audience for each one. Most of all, I tried to be there for them in their different seasons of life. Now I am enjoying the love of my seven grandchildren.

I can still see that little boy on the side of that house with the paint peeling off. At this point in my life, I wanted to see him smile at me. But he's not smiling. It's like he is saying, "What about all the other little boys like us? What are you going to do about them?"

My answer to that question is "The MANTOWN Project".

Part 1

Boys Are Born but Men Are Made ♂

What's the Problem?

The Assumption Problem

If you are a boy, when you reach a certain age, you are called a man. When you reach this age, you are expected to function in a responsible, mature, and beneficial manner that will contribute to society and the people around you. However, there is a problem. What is the problem? The problem is the assumption. What assumption? The assumption is that boys automatically grow up to be men. The assumption says that all you have to do to be a man, if you are a boy is eat, drink, and keep living. The assumption is if you live long enough to grow facial and pubic hair, be of the age that you can legally drink, and old enough to make a baby, you are a man.

In the mind of many in society boys automatically grow up to be men. This is the assumption. This assumption is harmful to boys because they are expected to be what they were never trained to be. Society is not acknowledging the fact that a boy must be developed into a man. The truth is "Boys are born but Men are Made." In order to be a man, you must not only be male (but you must be male), you must also have been taught truth, and be committed to growing in wisdom and be willing to apply the time-tested principles of life.

The Societal Problem

The problem is what happens to society when you, as a boy, never make it to what we call, ManTown. If you never make it to ManTown you become a menace to society. If you never become a real man, then <u>men, women</u>, and <u>children</u> will become your victims. A boy that was never taught and never committed himself to moral, ethical, and spiritual principles will be self-centered and cold. That boy will grow up to bring much pain and sorrow to those around him. Some of the products of grown adult males that were never taught, and trained ManTown Principles include, Narcissists, Sociopaths, Psychopaths, Alcoholics, and Drug Addicts. These problematic conditions can be seen in many males today.

The Elephant In The Room
"Male Issues"

MEN ARE CAUSING A LOT OF PAIN!!!

LYING

DISAPPOINTING PEOPLE THAT TRUST THEM

CHILDREN LEFT ABANDONED

CHEATING ON WIFE

DRUG ABUSE

GOING TO JAIL

CHILD ABUSE

STALKING

MURDERING WIFE & CHILDREN

DOMESTIC VIOLENCE

DRUNK DRIVING

FIGHTING

I'M GROWN! BUT WHAT'S A MAN?

NOBODY TOLD ME!!!

If we get no help we can become:
- Narcissist
- Sociopaths
- Psychopaths

Males grow up to be grown but "Men" are made through the Teaching & Training of Principles!

According to the National Statistical Domestic Violence Fact Sheet:
- One in three women have experienced severe physical violence from a man.
- In the United States, one in five women have been raped.
- In 2018, partner violence accounted for 20% of all violent crimes.

According to an article published in USA TODAY 12-6-22, in 2021 "Men commit 80% of all suicides in the United States. The Social Science & Medicine Vol 146, Dec. 2015, pages 249-256 reported that men are more likely than women to perpetrate nearly all types of interpersonal violence (e.g., intimate partner violence, sexual assaults, murder, binge drinking and drugs). The National Center for Health Statistics reports that in 2021 some 38,025 men committed suicide. The suicide rate is said to be four times as high for men as it was for women in 2021.

The percentage of men committing suicide tells us that men themselves are crying out for help. The U.S. Census Bureau reported almost 20 million children live without a father in the home. One in every four American kid lives without their biological fathers."

Some may conclude that "Men" are the problem. I wholeheartedly disagree! The problem is the failure to teach, train, and support our young boys, so they can learn to live by the life principles that prepares a boy to be a man.

What's the Solution?

The solution for addressing the question of whether you as a young boy will grow up to be a violent, irresponsible, angry, adult male is simple. Before you completely grow up and become set in your **"Little Baby Boy Thinking" LBT** ways, something must happen. You must be taught the time-tested moral, ethical, and spiritual principles of life. The wisdom and knowledge you receive from these principles will change your world view, give you purpose and meaning, impulse control, and strategies for behavior management. It will allow you to grow up and not just look like a man but literally act and behave like a real man.

Ideally, all these principles should have been learned through the teaching and example of your father. He would not only teach the principles to you but model these principles in his life before you, so that you could see them in action. However, if this opportunity has not been afforded to you in your life situation the next best solution is for "YOU" to study this material. You should study this material and let it become apart of your life. This material will allow you to grow to understand those crazy emotions you feel. It will help you understand why you desire to do the things that come across your mind to do. It will provide insight into many of the problems you are facing now, or you are soon to face. It will show you how to handle and respond to hard times, disappointments, and setbacks in a healthy manner. This material is set to provide information, motivation, life skills, and training that can change your life forever.

One of the areas of training that is so desperately needed in the training of boys to be men is the art of communication. Most marriages fail because of the male's inability or failure to communicate. So many boys grow up with no clue of how to communicate their feelings or how to read and hear the emotional communication of others. This material will help you learn how to listen. It will help you learn to not only listen with your ears but also with your eyes and heart. It will then teach you how to properly respond in a healthy manner.

You will learn that one of the most empowering listening skills will be your ability to truly hear yourself. This will prevent you from having self-delusions. To put it another way, it will prevent you from lying to yourself. You can be honest about your mistakes, your flaws, and where you need to improve. You can give credit to others and still appreciate yourself for the efforts you made. The great philosopher Socrates once stated, "Man know thyself". You will never know yourself if you fail to listen to yourself. You must listen to yourself to correct yourself. You will find that everything you say to yourself may not be true. This material will help you get started with the task of effective communication with yourself and others.

This material will address:

THE ART OF COMMUNICATION
- **How to Control Desire and Passions**
- **Self-Control and Self-Regulation**
- **How to Address Anxiety and Depression**
- **Character Building**
- **Healthy Living**
- **Relationships**

Part 2

Stuck in "Little Boy Thinking"

Understanding "The Boy"
To Understand "The Man"

The very first thing that must be clearly understood is the difference between the way that boys think from the way that men think. I have labeled the general way a boy thinks as, "LBT". That acronym stands for **"Little Boy Thinking."** Little Boy Thinking is a slightly bigger version of **"Little Baby Thinking."**

Think of a little baby just born, sleeping in a crib. When the baby is hungry, he wants someone to feed him. The baby doesn't care if the mother is sick. The baby doesn't care if the father just lost his job and has no money. The baby doesn't care if it is three o-clock in the morning and the crying wakes up the whole house. The only thing that the baby is thinking about is what he wants and nothing else. Now, as a baby, we don't expect him to have learned how to be considerate of others. We don't expect the baby to know how to delay the desire for immediate gratification. We know that the baby has not learned the meaning of that special word we call "empathy". Which is the ability to understand and share the feelings of another. At this stage of life, the baby expects to be served and totally cared for. The older the baby gets the more parents and society try to teach the baby how to care for himself. One of the first things the parents do when the baby is old enough is teach him to feed himself. Parents teach the baby to hold his own bottle and eventually hold a spoon. Parents that changed their dirty diapers will strive to potty train the child.

Let's face it, babies are totally self-centered. They are only concerned about themselves. However, we have patience with the baby because we believe that this little baby thinking will soon gradually fade away. As little boys and girls grow older, they sometimes desire not to grow-up. Sometimes even though they have learned how to do many things for themselves and others they still think like a little baby. This is true for girls and boys, but for the purposes of this material we will concentrate on boys. Boys that don't let go of little baby thinking become even more self-centered. They also become lazy waiting for others to clean up after them. They are selfish and lazy because, just like the little baby, they expect others to serve, feed, cloth, shelter, and make them happy. Just like the little baby they expect not to do any work. "Little Boy Thinking "is just like little baby thinking because when the baby doesn't get what he wants he will throw a tantrum. Those stuck in "Little Boy Thinking" will do the same when they don't get what they want.

L B T
"Little Boy Thinking"

What is Little Boy Thinking (LBT)?

The mind of a "Little Boy" is different than the mind of a mature "Man". Little Boy Thinking is totally focused on himself.

THE DIFFERENCE BETWEEN "THE BOY" AND "THE MAN"

There are three (3) main issues that differs between the boy and the Man:

WHAT LITTLE BOYS WANT:

▸ All they want is to play
▸ All they want is to eat
▸ All they want is to rest or sleep
▸ All they want is to have fun
▸ All they want is to do nothing

OBJECT:
The only object of real concern is his own "Self"

WHAT LITTLE BOYS DON'T WANT:

▸ They don't want to be told what to do.
▸ They don't want rules.
▸ They don't want responsibilities.

CONCERN:
The major concern of the "Little Boy" is how he can please himself.

▸ He is not considerate of other people's feelings.
▸ He is not concerned about cost or consequences.

BECOMING A MAN - STARTS WITH A CHANGE OF MIND!

The Man Town Letters

The Process: How A Boy Becomes A Man

Let's See how a little precious baby boy comes into this world. A woman automatically produces EGGS in her body if all things are normal. Each egg has the capacity or potential of becoming a human being, a newborn baby.

However, not one egg produced by a WOMAN will ever become a LIFE, a HUMAN, a BABY, unless that EGG comes in CONTACT with, is FERTILIZED by, and SPENDS DEVELOPMENTAL TIME with the SEED (SPERM) that comes from a MAN. The miracle of life takes place when the EGG and the SEED (SPERM) come together either through sexual intercourse or artificial insemination.

The egg must receive the seed then the baby starts to grow and develop. As the baby grows the Woman or Girl's stomach start to enlarge. The process will be complete in nine months if there are no complications the baby will then be delivered.

When a boy is born, he has a functional mind, if all things are normal. Within his mind is the

• The Seat of His Little Boy Thoughts.

• The Seat of His Little Boy Emotions.

We Will Call The Little Boy's Mind The EGG

This boys' mind has the potential of one day giving birth to the thoughts and emotions of a man. But just as a woman's egg must come in contact with, be fertilized by, and spend time with a man's seed to Create Life (**BABY**), there is something that must come in contact with the mind of a boy. A boy's mind must come in contact with, be fertilized by, and have developmental time with what I call "The Principles of Life to create (**MAN**)". The principles of life could be condensed to the three terms Wisdom, Knowledge, and Understanding, but we shall give more specifics.

If the principles of life never come in contact with the boy's mind and develop, then over time the boy will grow and become grown. However, a man's mind he will never have; therefore, a man he would never be. This boy will become a grown male with a little boy's mind.

If you can understand the process of human development, you will understand the process that allows the boy to miraculously become a man.

Embracing The Time-Tested Principles That Are The Proven Ingredients To Being A Man

What Are Some of These Principles?
Do No Harm!

The first principle addresses a person's intent and actions. Within this principle is the implication of a pure heart that has no guile. The idea of living a life with no ill will is the idea of living a life that is sensitive to the needs and values of others. To "Do No Harm," describes the humble man. It describes not only one able to talk but also to listen. This principle is the exact opposite of the bully. The bully says, I do what I want, and take what I want, regardless of who gets hurt. Some people are so twisted that they think it's funny to see people in pain.

Weinstein suggest this first principle "Do No Harm," is the most important. Can you imagine living in a society where everyone is looking to hurt you or to take what you have? A society that disregards this principle is cruel and corrupt. A society such as this will sexually use you to satisfy themselves, or simply hurt you for the fun of it.

There may be times that a boy may get punished when he is being disciplined or a person fired from a job. It hurts to get punished, and no one wants to get fired. However, the principle could best be understood as doing no harm for harm's sake, or only doing those things that are meant to help someone even if sometimes what is done may hurt. When a boy receives discipline, it should be motivated out of love for the child and done in an appropriate manner. Being fired from a job should be an understood consequence that comes from personal behavior and not because of a mean-spirited boss.

Do no harm is a general attitude that says, if I cannot help you, I will not purposely hurt you. If you are hurt in the short term, it is only because I believe it will do you good in the long run. If early in life a boy embraces this principle it will bring him peace and a life of no regret or remorse. One of the reasons some seek to do harm is because of the desire to win at everything.

Winning becomes so important that anything or anyone that threatens to interfere with winning becomes an object of hate and a target of revenge. From these emotions comes the desire to do harm. At the end of a running play in football

we can sometimes see the fruit of an attitude that puts winning before everything. The running back has been tackled and he is on the ground. The linebacker that tackled him, pretending to get up, holds on to the running back's leg and gives a quick twist, because he wants to put this running back out of the game even if it takes cheating to do it. However, if a person holds to the principle of, "do no harm," that person would have the attitude, if I cannot win fairly, then I do not want to win at all.

Make Things Better

In most people I believe it fair to say that it is good character to want to make an impact on the world we live in. That same instinct drives us to want to make this world a better place. Anyone that has genuinely helped someone in need would have a hard time denying that good warm feeling that comes over us when we serve others. The definition of character is the idea of a mark or engraving. We all want to make our mark on the world we live in.

We impact our families, schools, and our communities. Early on we can observe the kind of impact we are making. The principle, "Make Things Better," if followed will move our decisions toward helping instead of hurting, giving instead of taking and serving instead of stealing. When "Make Things Better," becomes an important principle in our lives we start doing two things.

1. We check ourselves and begin to closely consider what we do and say.
2. We try to be the best we can be in everything we do.

We know that the better we are the more we will be able to do. Our desire to make things better motivates us to serve. The basic question we ask ourselves is what do I enjoy doing that will also be beneficial to the world I live in? The basic attitude is whatever I am apart of I want to do my part to make things better. It is all about being my best self for the good of all concerned.

Respect Others

Being respected carries the idea of deserving high regard and honor. If you believe all men were created equal and endowed by their creator to pursue life, liberty and to pursue happiness, then you start off with the foundation to respect all men.

This principle has a great deal to do with the amount of value we give humanity as a whole. The less we value human life the easier it is to show disregard and outright disrespect for others. This same value system will also affect our own self-concept, and personal integrity. The word respect suggests the ability to see that all people are special. If we do not respect ourselves, we can never truly respect others.

Respect

I respect you
You respect me
A beautiful world this is gonna be
(Repeat Chorus)

Verse 1

I don't cuss, you don't cuss me
We sit down we talk about it sensibly
You do your job and I'll do mine
Responsibility it is no crime
(Repeat Chorus)

Verse 2

You have your needs I can truly see
But please respect a girl's morality
Go find your wife – leave mine alone
By the help of my God we make a beautiful home
(Repeat Chorus)

Verse 3

Good food for the body
You wash it with soap
You don't destroy it with the deadly dope
It makes no difference if you're
Black or white, we all must learn how to the thing right
(Repeat Chorus)

Artist: Willie B. Williams Jr.

Weinstein summarizes this important ingredient of respect. He stated,

"Each of us benefits by taking the principles of respect for others seriously. By honoring our responsibilities to tell the truth, keep our promises, maintain confidentiality, and remain trustworthy, we give a gift to all those with whom we have a relationship. By enriching others, we enrich ourselves."

The bridge that leads us to the land of respect for others is really just to have love for all mankind. This love makes us care about the rights of others.

Our love will drive us to tell the truth. The more we tell the truth and keep our promises the more we are seen as trustworthy. The meaning of trustworthy is simply being worthy of confidence and able to be depended on. Respect for others builds people's confidence in us.

When bullies talk about getting respect, they are really talking about something different. When they talk about respect, they are just talking about people being so afraid of them that they do whatever they say. Respect obtained through fighting and fear is short lived. Someone has said, "If you live by the sword you shall die by the sword."

Be Fair

Fairness is the offspring of Justice.

...But that's not fair! This is the cry of children all over the world. If the desire for fairness is not said it is felt. Somehow, we all seem to have a basic desire for fairness.

My one-year-old granddaughter was playing with a toy. Her two-year-old brother came and snatched the toy away from her. She could not speak words, but her body language and facial expression said clearly, "what just happened to me was not fair." Even though fairness is a basic desire, being fair is not always the easiest thing to do.

The Bible character Solomon was considered one of the wisest men that ever lived. One of the ways his wisdom was demonstrated was his ability to make fair judgments when people came before him with their disagreements. The best way to increase the ability to be fair is to strive to learn the laws of right and wrong, good and bad. I suggest the study of the Bible.

Be Loving

Regardless of how we try, we cannot get pass the absolute need for love. It is not hard to forgive if you love, even when your sister or brother does something that really hurts.

An old song that is still sung today is "What the world needs now is love…" One definition of Love is a genuine regard for the welfare of another. Love is not just a feeling. Love is a commitment that demands time and sacrifice. Love should be the motivating factor that connects a man to his responsibilities.

Love should be the drive that forces a man to provide and protect. A love for mankind is the foundation of heroes and heroines. The Bible records the internal attributes of real love. It is love that purifies, that gives substance, and provides a noble purpose to all we do or say.

*I Corinthians 13:1-8 Answer Three Fundamental Questions About Love:
- How valuable are my deeds without Love?
- How does Love act or behave?
- How can love be present in my life?

What Love Is and What It Does:
- It is kind and does not envy others.
- It is humble and not prideful.
- It is giving and not selfish.
- It is patient and not easily angered.
- It rejoices in doing right and not in doing wrong.

- It seeks to tell the truth not to tell lies.
- It never gives up, never loses faith, and hopes until the end.

Seek Knowledge

One of the foundational principles of being a man is knowledge. Men are called upon to lead, guide, and instruct. To be an effective leader, guide or instructor one must have knowledge. The opposite of knowing is not knowing and not knowing is ignorance. The real man is not content to dwell in ignorance. For this reason, a real man is a lifelong seeker of knowledge. He never stops learning. He does not mind learning because he knows sooner or later, he will need the knowledge. The real man knows good intentions are not good enough.

The lives of his love ones and those that follow him will be greatly affected by his example, advice, and directions. He knows that he will never know it all, so he takes two important steps. First, he learns how to find the  knowledge he may not possess. He seeks this knowledge in books, people of knowledge, or the environment. Secondly, he connects moral values and principles in his new found knowledge before making his decisions. Finally, he organizes his knowledge for future use.

Show Wisdom

According to the Webster's Dictionary to be wise is to be marked by deep understanding, keen discernment, and a capacity for sound judgment. To have wisdom is to be sensible, sane, and just. To have wisdom is to possess the ability to make good solid decisions. To be without knowledge is to be ignorant. To be without wisdom is to be foolish. The real man is not content to be ignorant and is certainly nobody's fool.

Having wisdom and showing wisdom is two different things. An individual may have a clear understanding and possess the capability to make sound decisions and yet choose to do the complete opposite of what they know to do. Apart of the measure of a man is that he does what he has to do and not necessarily what he wants to do. Wisdom is not shown by just words. Wisdom is really shown by what a person does, and the decisions that are made.

Have Faith

Faith is believing in that which others may not see, and trusting in a hope that others may not have. It is faith that makes the impossible possible. Faith releases the energy and the power that is hidden in the human spirit. Someone has said "If you can believe it, you can achieve it." Show me a person that has no faith, and I will show a person who has no energy to make his dreams come true. A person that has no faith always makes excuses for why something cannot be done. A person with no faith will always try to stop those who do believe. People that have no faith are the ones that make fun of people with faith in order to feel better about not trying or for not doing anything themselves.

Faith must be directed inward and outward. In other words, a man must have faith in himself and the capacity to believe in the people and possibilities around him. A good place to start is to have faith in God, and that man was created in his image. To believe that all men were created equal by God and in his image is to acknowledge the limitless possibilities afforded to man because he serves a limitless God. This faith also directs one's hopes and deeds toward doing those things that are noble and just.

Be Courageous

The following is a true story about a young fellow who allowed his friends to talk him into disobeying his conscience:

Before John changed his life, he would drink beer and get drunk with his friends. After he became a aware that he need to change, things were different. He no longer wanted to go with his friends and drink beer. His old friends didn't like this, so they begged John and teased him until he gave in and started drinking beer again with them.

One night John and his friends were drinking. They had a terrible accident. The car in which they were riding turned over and smashed. John's back was broken just below the neck.

John spent many days and nights in the hospital. Now John uses a wheelchair to get around. He will never walk again. This tragedy would not have happened if John had just said "No."

Just say "NO"

As you grow up, you will face many temptations. You may be offered drugs and told about the "great feeling" you will have when you take them. Just say "No." (Be sure to tell an adult whom you can trust about any situation in which you have been offered drugs.)

Someone you know may try to get you to smoke. Just say, "No." A friend may try to get you to drink beer or wine or some other alcoholic beverage. Just say, "No." You may have friends who are involved in these things, and they may try to get you to join them, but just say, "No." The Bible says, "My son, if someone entice you (try to get you to do wrong), consent thou not (don't do it!)." (Proverbs 1:10)

According to Webster, courage is mental and moral strength. It is the strength to withstand danger, to face fear, and hold up under adversity. A real man must be strong enough to take criticism from friends and enemies. Whenever an individual tries to do what is good, right, and moral, criticism is sure to follow. Courage is not always the absence of fear, but rather the willingness to work through fear to do what should be done. Courage is needed on so many levels. You will definitely need physical, moral, psychological, and spiritual courage if you are ever to reach the true status of being a man.

A man needs courage to fight for what's right, but he needs as much or even more courage to walk away from a fight. When marriage gets tough it is easier to walk away than fight through the problems and make it work. The fighting that must take place in this situation is  the willingness to calm down, discuss, communicate, compromise, and forgive to save your marriage. However, sometimes when a man feels mistreated and wants to physically strike back, he must demonstrate the moral courage to walk away.

REAL: Respected, Empowered, Appreciated, Loved

To become a real man a boy needs to understand what his real motivations are. Why are Pro-Athletes, Movie Stars, Doctors, Lawyers, Singers, Dancers, and even Gang Leaders and Pimps appealing to so many? The boy must understand that it is not the position that makes the jobs so appealing it is what having the position promises that makes it so attractive. I have identified these basic promises in the form of a single word, "REAL." We all want to be real. Each letter in the word represents a promise.

R – We want to be Respected.
E – We want to be Empowered.
A – We want to be Appreciated.
L – We want to be Loved.

"Be Real * For Real"

Let us look at the professional Athlete. He is respected because of the level of his achievements in the field of athletics. He is empowered by his opportunity to do what he does best. The fans, through attendance, applause and sometimes gifts and money, show appreciation for what this athlete does. The only area that this athlete may not be absolutely sure of is being unconditionally loved. However, some mistakenly think they have achieved the love they seek in adoring fans and massive applause.

 ## Respected

The boy must understand why respect is so important to all people. To be respected speaks to our very soul. Respect acknowledges and confirms our very existence. Respect says to a person you are not invisible. It not only reaffirms the presence of a person but also assures value in that presence. Take for example, if an individual looked in a mirror and saw no reflection this would be cause for great concern. Or if that same person looked in a mirror and the reflection was a hideous monster. This would be very disturbing. When people look at you and smile, they tell you two things. First, they acknowledge your existence, and second, they tell you your presence is pleasing and welcome. In other words, your presence is a good thing. The eyes of a person becomes our mirror. We trust the message of some people's eyes more than others.

Some people train themselves not to look in the eyes of others so that they will not risk the possibility of negative demeaning messages. While they may be able to ignore many, their need to be affirmed will drive them to find assurance somewhere, even if it is just in the eyes of an animal. It is difficult to interact or even stand before people that make no acknowledgment of your presence. To be overlooked and discounted, especially when you feel you deserve consideration,

is to experience disrespect. We feel respected when we are warmly received. We feel respected when provisions are made to treat with care those things that belong to us and are connected with us such as parents, family, religion, our possessions, or affiliations such as our team or country.

You must understand the difference between genuine respect and fake respect. You must learn the difference between earned respect and phony respect. Time tested Principles produce real respect. The principles cannot be denied. People that show disrespect to those who actively work the principles must struggle themselves with guilt and shame.

If eyes give the reflection to a good presence, and they do; the young boy working the principles will be able to trust the eyes of the one he sees in the mirror. He will look in the mirror and see himself. He must learn to feel good about himself when he knows he is doing right and good. Even when he makes mistakes, he must see himself as a work in progress.

You must also learn that there are those who would use an individual's need for respect for their own advantage. They know the need people have to be recognized. They know the need people have for acceptance. They use these needs as bargaining chips. They withhold their recognition and acceptance until a person bends to their will. They basically say I refuse to recognize you or accept you until you meet my standards or do what I say. You must learn to recognize when people try to use fake respect on you and don't fall for it.

Fake respect is the kind of acceptance and recognition that is unfair, unjust, and sometimes abusive aggression. This kind of respect is sought after by the bully and abusive father or husband. They think respect is scaring people into doing whatever they say or else they will hurt you. You must learn real respect begins within. Look in the mirror and accept yourself with all your mistakes and flaws and still know that what God made is good.

Empowered

Understand why empowerment is so important to all people. To be empowered speaks. It says a person has the opportunity to be good and productive. It also says a person is worthy of one of man's greatest longings and that longing is the longing to be free. Something inside any normal individual is the desire to master and manage their environment. Babies from birth tackle the task of getting around and feeding themselves. When they first come into this world if they are to get from point A to point B they must be carried. If they are to receive nourishment it must be provided to them, or they will die. An individual's DNA programs the physical and psychological development to gradually move from total dependence to independence.

The task of being mobile carries with it the promise of empowerment. It promises the individual that the power of getting around will be determined by self and not dependent on others.

The baby naturally strives to move from crawling to walking and then to running. It then moves to driving and from driving to flying. We not only want to do these things, we want to master them. The better we do these things the more empowered we feel and the better we feel about ourselves. When we master one thing, we feel free to strive to master other things. To some degree empowerment is the same as freedom. To be empowered is to know that we have the freedom to come and to go, make decisions for ourselves, and pursue our dreams. It also says that we possess the confidence that we can do what we do well.

You must learn to reject the temptation and the slavery of the "Baby syndrome", (Avoiding empowerment to remain dependent on others). Even thou slavery is contrary to the human spirit its benefits can be tempting. One of the temptations of slavery is the fact that the slave is to simply do what he or she is told. Therefore, the slave does not have to think or make responsible decisions. In fact, the good slave is encouraged not to think at all, simply follow directives. You find this slave mentality in gang members when they are given a gun and told to go out and kill somebody for nothing.

This attitude is also found in those that will do anything they see the crowd do. The salve mentality gladly assigns the responsibility of all behavior to someone or something else. For example, someone may say, "I ran over the child, but I am not responsible because I was drunk," or "I'm not responsible for what I have done because the devil made me do it.

These attitudes are all a part of what I call the 'Baby Syndrome". In the baby syndrome parents are expected to provide food, clothing, and shelter and make sure the baby is happy. Many adult males still expect parents to feed, clothe, and provide shelter for them. Many so called "Players," use women to take care of them. They spend the money, drive the cars, and live in the homes of women because they have not matured enough to accept the responsibility for themselves. They act empowered when in reality they are still dependent babies.

Everyone faces periods when they need help to get on their feet because of hard times. However, no real man is content to stay or live in a dependent state. A real man must be free and empowered. The other side of empowerment is the need to make sure that one's empowerment remains subject to that individuals' principles. Empowerment is not license to do harm, be unloving, unfair, or be disrespectful. The real man seeks empowerment for the purpose of living true to his principles.

Appreciation

You must understand why appreciation is so important to all people. Appreciation speaks. It says you exist, and you are valued. It says you have contributed to your world. It says you are not just a parasite that takes but you are a producer that gives. Appreciation says whatever the actions, works or deeds that may have been done;

they were profitable and well received. Many times, people value appreciation more than money. History is filled with examples of people that had all the money they would ever need, go out of their way to help others desiring no more than a simple, thank you. The sacrifices and troubles one endure for others are not considered in vain when appreciation is shown.

The act of appreciation is at the same time the act of recognition. Just as respect says you exist so too does appreciation. If a person is appreciated that means that person has done something, and if the person did something then the person must exist. To further this thought appreciation says whatever was done was good, which suggests that the person's existence is good. When we see others appreciated, a spark of hope assures us that one day we will receive that same thing. The professions that add value to the lives of others receive this type of appreciation.

You must be taught and learn not to seek appreciation. Learn to serve and let appreciation come if it will. Appreciate the opportunity to be productive and to make valuable contributions. Understand that we enrich our own lives when we enrich the lives of others. You must be forewarned that many of your good deeds and services may be ignored or be received with no thanksgiving at all. You must not be discouraged or dismayed. Learn to accept the human faults of others and do right because it is good to do right. You must learn true appreciation comes after, sacrifice, benevolence, or service and not before.

Love

You must understand why love is so important to all people. Love is important because of what it says. Appreciation says I show favor, care, and admiration towards you because of what you do or what you have done. Love says, I cleave to you, show you favor simply because you are. Love is the most fundamental need in all of humanity. It crosses the lines of race, gender, and economic status. It crosses the national borders of every country in the world.

Love affirms man's inner worth and value. This is why a mother's love is thought to be so valuable. No matter what a child may have done, the reputation of the mother is to say, "That's my child, and I love my child." The love man longs for is unconditional love. Mankind seeks this love from the cradle to the grave. The need for love is first apparent in babies. The baby's physical and emotional development is severely affected if the baby does not feel love interpreted through the acts of affection. Some of these acts that can be interpreted as love are cuddling, caressing, smiling, and playing. Babies display a sense of well-being and security when they feel love. However, the baby may display withdrawal or even aggressive behavior when these acts of affection are withheld.

The Human spirit has a need to be close to other human beings not just physically, but also emotionally. This is why going to prison is not only an effort to protect society, but it is also a punishment. When man is isolated from other human beings, such as in solitary confinement, a person can literally lose their mind. This great need for bonding, showing, and receiving favorable regard has caused people to make great sacrifices and risk everything they possess. The largest percentage of suicides can be traced back to the thought, "nobody loves me, and I am all alone." Love cannot be bought or sold. Love is not earned; it is simply given.

The Greeks identified the different kinds of love. There is Romantic Love that is shown to a mate. There is friendship love that would identify a friend. There is Family Love. However, supreme love is Godlike or (Agape) unconditional love. Not only is this love unconditional love, but it is seeking the good of the other over self. The different kinds of love should all be regulated by this agape love.

You should know the importance of having a strong faith that affirms your belief in a loving God. The God you need to know is the God that will love and accept you when all others have forsaken you. You must have a faith that acknowledges the fact that God wants you to do right but will also forgive and restore you if you fall short.

"Be Real * For Real"

Respected + Empowered + Appreciated + Loved

 Learn how to have realness within. Don't try to obtain realness from the profession you seek. You bring realness to the profession. Do not seek respect, empowerment, appreciation, or love from your profession. Bring to your profession personal acknowledgment, an internal power, a self-appreciation produced by pure motives, hard work, and the knowledge of a divine love that will never let you down.

The boy should select his vocation based on aptitude, ability, need and satisfaction. However, he must be in touch with the fact that certain professions are attractive to him because they seem to promise Respect, Empowerment, Appreciation and Love. Some professions that seem to promise these things are:

*Movie Stars	*Rappers	*Politicians	*Pro-Athletes	*Singers
*Gang Leaders	*Lawyers	*CEO's	*Dealers (Dope)	
*Preachers	*Doctors	*Dancers	*Pimps	

Many inner-city youths choose the profession that promises the most respect with the easiest requirements (i.e. – Pimps, Gangs, and Dealers). It must be remembered that some professions must be avoided at all costs because they are in complete opposition to the principles a real man must live by. For example, being a dope dealer will do harm, make things worse for many, does not show respect, demonstrate no love and is totally unfair to the innocent naive soul caught in its web. The innocent soul might be a baby addicted to dope through its mother before it is even born.

You must be taught and know that certain conditions and situations are desirable, but none of these conditions has the power to make one REAL. The following conditions cannot fulfill a true realness.

Financial Riches   **Unrestricted License**

National Fame   **Educational Degrees**

Controlling Power   **Physical Attractiveness**

Respected vs Financial Riches

Those things that we look for within the word respect are (1) acknowledgment, (2) attention, (3) favorable recognition and (4) valued regard. Financial riches will open the door to all of these desired reactions. When a person has an excessive amount of money they receive acknowledgment, attention, favor, recognition and what they say is highly valued. However, there is a huge difference in being personally respected versus the respect received brought primarily because of financial ability.

Being personally respected because of who you are versus being respected for what you have is the same as owning and driving your own luxury car verses being a hitchhiker picked up off the side of the road and allowed to ride in one. When you are personally respected the respect goes home with you. It is yours when you sleep and when you get up in the morning.

When you are respected for what you have, the respect is not yours, it belongs to and will always belong to the money or material possessions you have. It is the dollars, not you that is receiving the attention and favorable regard. As long as you are permitted to ride in the same car with the dollar you can vicariously enjoy the benefits. However, all of those benefits end when your hitch-hiking ride is over. It is then you come to realize you had never been respected. Many become bitter when they realize it was the money that was being respected all of the time. Seek to be respected for who you are, not for what you have.

Empowered vs Financial Riches

Those things that we look for within the word empowered is (1) Power, (2) Freedom, (3) Competence, and (4) Opportunity. Financial riches will open the door to all of these desires except one. The one thing financial riches cannot give to the person that has been empowered through financial riches is competence. Money is so respected by people that they will take a backseat to the dollar. If you have the dollar, you may be fooled to think the dollar has made you important. This may deceive you into having an unstable sense of power. The people that run after the dollar are content to allow the holder of the dollar to remain in this delusion.

You may wonder what is good about having money. Money will allow you freedom to do and to go. Money will allow an individual the privilege and opportunity to try. Money can permit the person that has absolutely no singing ability to perform on stage before the most prestigious audience. However, it cannot erase the quiet murmurs that say this person cannot sing. Money cannot buy you talent and ability.

As much as financial riches bring freedom, it also brings dependence. Financial riches demand competent management. This has been demonstrated by those that became fast millionaires one year and within one or two years they are completely broke and embarrassed. Many sport figures and movie stars have faced the unforgiving consequences of people handling their money that just did not know what they were doing. People they trusted and depended on showed themselves untrustworthy or totally incompetent. They made serious errors in judgment that sometimes resulted in the loss of fortunes.

The War Against Narcissism

Some psychologists believe this disorder is acquired by way of genetics. However, no gene or cluster of a genetic system has yet been discovered to rule out the role of nurture plus nature. There may be a percentage that are disposed to personality disorders from birth, however, I believe that a person's environmental exposure and upbringing plays a significant role in many that would be diagnosed NPD.

If you as a boy allow LBT (Little Boy Thinking) to continue to control your mind, you may become a victim of a terrible psychological condition called "Narcissism". The disorder is known as the Narcissistic Personality Disorder. Narcissism is like a grown-up person with a little baby mindset and desires. The little baby loves attention and desires to be taken care of. The little baby has no consciousness of other people's concerns. When a little baby doesn't get what it wants it will cry, kick, scream, and throw tantrums. However, as an older person the tantrums and meltdowns are much bigger and much more destructive. As an older person you are more intelligent. You employ more tricks to get attention, more cunning tricks to get what you want, and more power to inflict pain on those who refuse to serve you as you desire. You also have the skill and the will to lie, deceive, manipulate, and exploit others to get what you want. This condition will never allow you to truly be happy because inside your heart you are always afraid. You are afraid, insecure, and need the approval of the very ones you hurt and abuse.

You, like many boys, may be experiencing some hard and disappointing, even painful things in your life. You may feel less valued than others and unfairly treated. If there is no one there to help you through these times, you may be about to make a decision. You may decide to forget about everyone else and just look out for yourself. You may decide that the only one that matters in this world is you. I remember a book that was entitled, "Looking Out for Number One". Even now your heart may be getting cold and numb. If you make the decision to forget about others and only care about what you want, how you feel, and what you like, something will happen to you. Over time you will develop what some people call a "Hard-Heart" and become "Cold-Blooded". If you focus on yourself and your selfish desires, there are some things you may never learn.

- You may never learn how to truly love anyone but yourself.
- You may never learn to have "empathy" which is the ability to understand and be concerned about the pain of others.
- You may never learn to be responsible and hold yourself accountable for bad behavior.
- You may never learn to serve and not just be served.
- You may never learn how valuable you are as a person, and that you don't have to brag, show off or lie to be important.

The terrible thing about this condition is that once you really get it, you don't know you have it. When you are really self-centered and narcissistic you think you are normal and everyone else has the problem. You genuinely think you are better than everyone else. You think others are just jealous of you. You think you deserve special treatment because everyone on earth is here to serve you. You don't mind hurting other people to get what you want because other people's feelings don't matter. When you have truly become self-centered and narcissistic, you laugh when you see others cry. Many times, you just feel nothing at all. You can't love others because you don't even know how.

To rid yourself of this disorder once you truly have it is almost impossible to do. This is why it is so important to start working on preventing this disorder at an early age. The DSM – 5 (The Diagnostic Statistical Manual of Mental Disorders) states that narcissism has its beginnings in adolescence and early adulthood.

You may be headed in that direction right now. This is why I am excited that you have decided to study this material at this point in your life. It is possible for you to turn your life around before selfishness becomes part of your basic character and you feel helpless to change.

Here are some tools used by the "Narcissists" to get their way:

- Lies – A self-centered person believes that it is alright to lie if it gets him what he wants.
  (Truth) – The truth is when you lie you destroy all the trust people have in you. They stop believing you. You get the reputation of being a liar.

- Deception – A self-centered person uses tricks to try and make people think they are something they are not for approval or to take advantage.
  (Truth) – When you try to make people believe you are something that you are not, they come to see you as a fake and a phony.

- Manipulation – A self-centered person will try to use people with no intention of doing right in order to get what they want.
  (Truth) – Many times what you do to others often comes back to hurt you. The principle, "You reap what you Sow" is true.

- Temper – A narcissist will sometimes use rage, anger, and temper-tantrums to get their way. They will bully and threaten people that they perceive are in their way.
  (Truth) – One day someone will refuse to be bullied. Sooner or later, someone will come along to fight for justice.

- Enticements – A self-centered person may try to control people by giving things like money, favors, and positions. To get things to go their way they threaten to take these things away or use bribery.

(Truth) – The self-centered person knows that when they run out of things people will leave. He will know there is no love or security. They can never trust that someone genuinely loves them for themselves.

ManTown Thinking – (MTT)

Now that you can see and understand how a little boy thinks, it is time to see how a "Man" thinks. I want to introduce you to "ManTown Thinking". To make it simple "ManTown Thinking is thinking and being responsible for yourself and others.

The first question that would be asked by a little boy is, "What do I want?". However, the first question asked by the Man Town Man is, "What do others need?". The little boy seeks and expects others to provide and serve him but the "Man Town Man" seeks to provide for and serve others.

A 'ManTown Man" is the product of learning and then living the time-tested moral, ethical, and spiritual principles of life. A "Man Town Man" is brought up on a steady diet of the Words of Wisdom. Much wisdom can be found in the bibles' book of Proverbs. In fact, the whole bible is a good place to find wisdom. The "ManTown Man" is secure enough in himself and what he stands for to be able to **listen** and **follow**, and yet wise and knowledgeable enough to **lead** and **guide**. He does not lead like the "Cowboy" that uses the whip and a gun to drive cattle. He leads like the "Shepherd" that has gained the love and confidence of the sheep so that when they hear his voice they follow.

A good way to understand how a "Man Town Man" thinks is to compare "LBT" with "MTT". Doing so will reveal a clear difference in focus and view.

The "LBT" (Little Boy Thinking) focus is on:
* What I Like
* What I Want
* What I Feel
* What I Need

The "MTT" (Man Town Thinking) focus is on:
- What Do Others Need
- How Can I Be of Service
- How Can I Make Things Better

The "LBT" (Little Boy Thinking) Vision is:
- To only see what is going on in the moment.
- To only be concerned about immediate gratification.
- To refuse to consider the impact on others.

The "MTT" (Man Town Thinking) Vision is:
- To consider what is needed now and for the future.
- To know the consequences that actions bring.
- To look for what can be done today to improve tomorrow.

The "ManTown Man" looks out for the benefit of others. He provides direction for himself and others. He identifies patterns to follow and pitfalls to avoid.

Part 3

ManTown Men "Build Safe Houses"

The Power of Being Safe

I have discovered the power of the concept of "Safety". I would go so far as to say that without feeling safe it is impossible to live a happy life. The absence of safety opens the door to every bad thing we can imagine. The absence of safety brings fear and terror, nightmares and screams, fighting and depression, anxiety, greed, stealing, suicide and murder.

The real mission of the "ManTown Man" is to build a house of safety for himself and those in the sphere of his influence. The "Man Town Man" build Safe Houses.

"ManTown Men" Build
a Safe House For Themselves

Human beings were created with three main parts. Human beings have a mind, a body and a spirit. Each one of those areas must be safe for a person to have peace and be happy. A person must feel safe physically, mentally, and spiritually. You are probably familiar with the problems that come from feeling unsafe physically and mentally, however, we also have the need to feel safe spiritually. This is sometimes referred to as existential anxiety. You feel anxious about fate and death. You feel empty and meaningless. It is your spiritual sense of safety that allows you to see life has purpose and meaning.

The "Man Town Man" first learns to take responsibility to protect these areas in his own life and then seeks to help others with theirs.

The "ManTown Man" seeks to take care of his body. He knows that his body is a gift. His desire to eat right, exercise and rest is not because of arrogance or boastful pride but simple appreciation. He knows that his body is his house, and he just wants to make it safe.

The "ManTown Man" develops his mind. He knows that his mind must be protected from one of its greatest enemies. The enemy of the mind is ignorance. Ignorance will destroy the mind and body. He knows an ignorant foolish man ends up poor, in prison, or in the graveyard. He knows his mind needs wisdom, knowledge, and understanding. The "Man Town Man" develops a strong intelligent mind as a part of his safe house.

The "ManTown Man" understands the need for a spiritual faith. I suggest the Christian faith. There will be problems and situations too heavy to bear and too hard to explain. To have a spiritual faith that can provide comfort, peace, and a sense of safety in times of trouble is of great importance. A person with a spiritual faith can find self-control and exercise composure when others around them are falling apart. I suggest the Christian Faith because it answers the existential questions of "Who am I?" "Why am I here?" "How am I to be?" and What's After This?"

In the Christian faith every person is made in the image of God and is loved by God. This says to every individual that your existence is not accidental, but intentional and meaningful. Not only were you created by God and loved by God, but you were made to be like God. According to the bible God is truth, love, merciful, just, and righteous. If you then are to be like God then you too will be honest, truthful, loving, merciful, fair and righteous. This is just to name a few of the positive traits man has been called to emulate. Some see the question of the hereafter answer in Christianity as problematic because of the idea that peace will come to those that live right and punishment for those that don't. Whether you chose to believe this or not it is still fair to say you will live a much more fulfilling, productive, and positive life if you live your life following the principles of honesty, peace and love. Spiritual faith also helps us realize in times of trouble that we don't have to be alone.

The "ManTown Man" understands he must constantly work on himself. Self-improvement for him is a way of life. He knows that a strong body, sharp mind, and a spiritual connection to a higher power will equip him with what he needs to help others. He understands that you must know how to swim if you want to be a lifeguard that helps those that are drowning.

The "ManTown Man" Builds a Safe House for His Family

One of the most important gifts given to a man is "The Seed of Life". At some point boys grow and develop the physical and biological ability to produce seed. The testosterone hormone is naturally dumped into a growing boy's bloodstream along with other hormones. These developmental chemicals and hormones will cause your hair to grow, the voice to change, and change the way you think and feel. You begin to see things differently. You notice things you've never noticed before and experience desires you never had before.

This is the time that a growing boy needs the guidance of the "Man Town Principles". This is the time you must be taught the value of the "Seed of Life". You must also be taught the awesome responsibility that comes with this gift. You must come to understand that this gift makes you the "Gate-Keeper of Life". You must come to understand that no one comes into this world without the seed of life. You must accept the fact that every life that comes into this world by your seed is your responsibility. You are to make safe anyone that comes into this world through your seed. It is at this time you must learn to value your seed and the potential life it may bring. You must learn to love and appreciate the potential life that it may bring. I am saying you must have a love for your child before it is born. Before this potential life comes you learn to demonstrate your love through being careful and prepared. You learn to care about the potential human being before you engage in casual relationships.

What I'm about to suggest is perhaps considered radical if not impossible. I suggest that you and all boys be taught and learn to gain impulse control. You should be taught and trained to control your instincts and passions for the good of all concerned. Parents potty-train babies, set eating and water breaks for little children to train them to control their normal impulses. Boys must also be taught this critical skill when facing puberty. You must understand your "Why" for the need to control your natural impulses and passions.

You must understand that the practice of self-control is to protect your own future. It will also protect your child from being aborted and lift the burden off the back of some young lady to make an unfair decision. You must be taught to love the possibility of having a child before he or she comes. At the same time, you know that there is the possibility that you may not have children. The motivation for your impulse control must then be that you know it is wise and morally right not to be sexually promiscuous. Casual sex has come back to haunt and hurt many men years and years later.

For you to understand the awesome privilege and the noble responsibility that is granted to a boy that becomes a man and is able to possesses the seed of life, I wrote this song. The song is entitled, "Seed Love". I hope this song starts a move-ment for all males. I would call it, "The ManTown Seed Celebration,". To have the power with the right woman to produce life is no small thing. It is something that should be celebrated not denigrated. It is something pure not dirty and nasty. It would be a movement where males would be protective and selective about how the seed is sown. It would be a movement that put Life before Lust and Love for your baby over just looking for a good time.

The "ManTown Man" Builds a Safe House for His Child

The "ManTown Man" is committed to building a safe house for his child be-fore his child comes into the world. This is why you must be concerned about being in a committed relationship that is stable and prepared for the coming of a child. Marriage to the mother of your child may sound old fashion, however, it is the best environment for your child. One of the best ways to prevent abortions is to only give your seed to the woman that has already committed her life to be the mother of your children.

When your child comes into this world, God, in His infinite wisdom, has al-ready assigned, through nature, that the two individuals involved in the child com-ing were to be the specific caretakers. This assignment was given to the seed-giver and the seed developer. The seed-giver is the man, and the seed developer is the woman. The "ManTown Man" that loves his wife knows that his first responsibil-ity is to provide a safe house for her, so that she can be a safe house for the child. When a woman is pregnant with a child, she was designed to be the child's safe house. She provides the child's shelter from the cold and the rain. She provides the child's food and nutrition. The child is never alone but is with the mother wherever she goes. The mother protects the child from outside hurt and harm. Ultimately, when the child is ready, she will direct the child by way of abdominal contractions to take its place in the world. In other words, she gives the child direction to live its own life.

The "ManTown Man "knows that as his wife is being a safe house for his child, he is responsible for making a safe house for her.

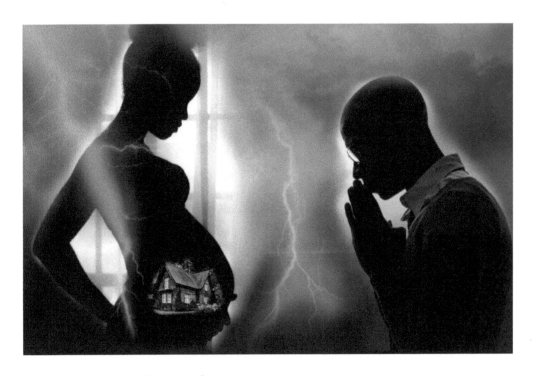

A Father Shows Love By Protecting
The Mother Who Is
The Safehouse Of Their Child

The same four areas of safety she is providing for the child are the same four areas he is to be providing for her. The "ManTown Man" knows that he can make his wife unsafe for the baby by the way he interacts with her. He knows that when his wife is worried, sad, frightened, and afraid stress hormones are released in her bloodstream. This makes things uncomfortable for the baby. If she is not getting the proper rest and nutrition these things are also unsafe for the child.

4 Major Categories That Threaten
A Family Safe House

First Major Categories Of Safe House Danger:
Loneliness
Isolation
Abandonment
Sense of Not Belonging

The "ManTown Man" will not be so busy working, making money or having fun that he neglects or forgets about his wife. He knows that he must earn a living, but he also realizes that this does not give him an excuse to abandon his wife. He strives to let her know that she is not alone. Isolation and solitary confinement are the worst punishment a person can receive. The 'ManTown Man" is committed to protecting his wife from this safe house danger.

The solution to this problem is sensitivity and vigilance. He knows he must read the emotions of his wife daily. He must not just assume everything is alright. He understands he must be prepared to be engaged at home and not just at work. He must get involved at home in conversation and service. He will give her the time and attention she needs to avoid the feelings of loneliness and abandonment.

Second Major Categories Of Safe House Danger:
Deprivation
Poverty
A Lack of Provisions

This can be a great challenge to the "ManTown Man" because we can't always control financial situations. However, he knows he is depended on to provide for

Seed Love

I don't know how old I was when I came to see
The greatest gift in the world had been given to me
It wasn't money, wasn't gold, it wasn't fortune or fame
It was the thought that my seed would be wearing my name
(Chorus)
I'm talking about seed love
Ohooo seed love
That's having your baby and then being there for your child
I'm talking about seed love
Ohooo seed love
I had my babies and then, I let my babies have me
I got to know my children and then, I let my children know me
(Verse)
All you guys going around saying you're so mad
Because you grew up all by yourselves, now your hating your dad
How in the world do you think, anyone will have pity
When you're throwing your seed, all over the city
(Chorus)
You need to learn seed love
Ohooo seed love, that's having your baby and then being there for
your child
I'm talking about seed love
Ohooo seed, seed love
I had my babies and then
I let my babies have me
I got to know my children and then
I let my children know me
The life of a man is in the seed and the seed of life is in the man.
Brother if you please do what you can to have seed love

his family. This motivates him to work hard and yet not forget his other responsibilities. This will cause him to have to make some very difficult decisions. He will be forced to do jobs to make ends meet. He may have to sacrifice or put on hold some childhood dreams. What keeps the "ManTown Man" going is his value system. He has placed family before self. He has decided to find the job to fit the family instead of forcing the family to fit the job. Providing basic needs should not be confused with getting everything we want. Decent shelter, clothing, food to eat, and transportation are considered basic needs. With proper management the other things will come.

Third Major Categories Of Safe House Danger:
Exposure to Danger
Physical
Emotional Abuse

The "ManTown Man" is a protector. He feels a natural responsibility to keep his home safe. He is vigilant and watchful about the danger in the environment in which his family lives. He not only protects his wife from physical, emotional, and verbal abuse of others, but he also protects her from his own physical and verbal abuse. He communicates with his wife in a healthy manner. He knows how to work together with his wife to make his home safe. He uses that same care to protect his children from physical and emotional abuse.

Fourth Major Categories Of Safe House Danger:
No Aim
No Purpose
No Direction
No Why

This is an area that is best served by faith in God. For those who believe in the bible and believe in God, you know "Why" you live the way you do. You are living to please the God you love. You know to please God you must:

- Love your neighbor as yourself and help others in need.
- Love your wife as Christ loved the church (He gave His life for her).
- Love your children and bring them up right.
- Be honest, faithful and true (no cheating).

Willie B. Williams

The ManTown Man...

- Will guide his family and give them a reason to live right and do right.
- Will rely on his faith in God for an example, standard, and guide to live by.
- Will be there for his family and strive to be someone they can trust and believe.
- Will build a safe house by giving his wife and children love, time and intentional attention.
- Will provide the provisions needed to live a good life.
- Will protect them, as much as he can, from the danger of emotional and physical abuse, not only from others but also himself.
- Will give them direction for their lives through his faith and example.

Part 4

Boys Must Reject the Lies

Reject The Lies

At an early age you must determine what you accept to be true and what you believe to be false. This is especially true as it relates to what you think will make you a man. You must decide what you truly think makes a boy a man. You must determine what you think you must have and what you must do that will ultimately allow you to be the man you were destined to be.

Growing up you will be told many things by parents, peers, friends, and even enemies about what it takes to be a man. What you believe and follow will determine if you ever make it to "ManTown". What you must always remember is that what it takes to be a man has never been determined by people but by principles. The moral, ethical and spiritual principles must be received and believed and practiced. These principles are supposed to be given to you by your parents and those that love you. However, sometimes you may receive information that is not true. Sometimes well-meaning friends or family may hand down to you things they were taught about what it takes to be a man. Unfortunately, what they were told and taught was just not true.

There are four lies (things often promoted about being a man) that you must understand are not true about what it takes to be a man. These false claims have caused many to live a life of disappointment and brought pain to the people in their lives.

The Four Lies to Be Rejected:

I.   The Biological Lie

II. The Chemical Lie

III. The Anti-Social Lie

IV. The Materialistic Lie

I. Reject The Biological Lie

There will be some who will tell you that, you are not a man until you have facial, chest, and pubic hair. Just having a mustache or a beard will be all it takes for some people to refer to you as a man. Some will claim you need big muscles if you want to be seen as a man. They will say, you must have six pack stomach muscles and a big chest for manhood respect. Finally, there are those that suggest having sexual relationships makes a boy a man. Some of your friends may look at you as if you have arrived when you claim to have had a sexual encounter.

These biological indicators, such as hair, muscles, and the ability to produce seed are only indicators of physical development. Nature and time (if you eat and live) will allow you to grow to be an adult male. Over time it just happens. It takes no learning at all to see a boy grow hair over time and over time produce seed. Over time a boy will become an adult male and look like a man. However, just looking like a man doesn't make you a man. The biology alone will not make you a man. It takes Nature and Nurture (Time and Teaching) for a boy to become a man. A "ManTown Man" is not just an adult male. A "ManTown Man" is an adult male that has been tried and trained in the time-tested moral, ethical, and spiritual principles. Biological development only gives you the outward shell of a man.

II. Reject the Chemical Lie

You must reject the chemical lie about being a man. The Chemical Lie about being a man has destroyed more potential men than all the world wars put together. The Chemical Lie has filled hospitals, graveyards, and divorce courts. What is the Chemical Lie? After all, a real man can handle his liquor.

Willie B. Williams

The Chemical Lie goes something like this:

You're not a "Man" until you:
- Take your first drink of alcohol.
- Can go buy liquor for yourself.
- Have gotten high on something.
- Go to clubs and drink socially.
- Are not afraid to try a new drug.

The Chemical Lie says to your ego that you are doing things only grown folks do. It says to your ego you are bold and daring. Know this, some people will cheer for you and act as if you did something great when you start drinking or getting high. The Chemical Lie is sometimes an unspoken cultural expectation. Your family and friends may just expect you to believe and participate. Your ego may be on the line if you don't drink or smoke with your friends. The Chemical Lie tells you that you show you are a man if you stand at a party with a drink in your hand. However, if you don't participate you may lose friends and must stand alone.

When you know what you believe and know why you believe it, it makes it easier to stand alone. Alcohol and drugs have destroyed millions of potential men. It has put them on street corners walking around broke and homeless. These chemicals that affect the mind, often do not make men but rather create helpless dependents that must be taken care of by others. Many males that look successful in business and Hollywood are addicted and helplessly dependent on drugs. Because these chemicals are promoted and funded by legal and illegal big business a great deal of time and money goes into convincing you to use them. They connect using these chemicals with being powerful, sexy, and tough. This is one of the biggest lies about being a man in the world. The use of these drugs creates false, temporary, and unreliable confidence. They cause people to do the exact things they have been taught not to do. Things like driving while drunk, becoming mean and starting fights, forcing their sexual desires on others, just to name a few. One thing is for sure, these chemicals can cause a person to be out of control and out of their right mind.

You may use these chemicals because you can, but do not be foolish enough to connect their use with being a "man".

III. Reject the Anti-Social Lie

Videos and Gangster Rap try to make it appear that a real man lives above the law. When I grew up, I knew a guy in high school. He was very popular. He was tough and had an "I don't care!" attitude. One day he was about to leave school to do something that was against the law. I happened to speak to him before he left. I confronted him about what he was about to do to try and convince him to change his mind. I said to him, "Don't you know that what you're about to do is against the law?" Then he said something to me that helped me understand how he thought and how his mind worked. He said to me, "I'm the law!". Basically, he told me that even though everybody else must obey and follow rules, he did not. He felt he did not have to obey rules because he was living in his "Little Boy" fantasy world that says, "Nobody tells me what to do!". The "little Boy" fantasy says, "I do whatever I feel like doing and no one can stop me!". This "LBT" (Little Boy Thinking) refuses to consider consequences. It refuses to consider consequences because in the little boy mind there should be no consequences. Many little boys, when they are told they can't do certain things make this statement, "I'll be glad when I get grown. Then I'll do whatever I want!"

Some of the Anti-Social Lies about being a man are as follows:

A. Fighting
  1. You are not a man if you don't fight when you get angry.
  2. You are not a man if you don't force people to do what you say.
  3. You are not a man if you don't take what you want.

B. Breaking The Law
  1. You are not a man if you're too afraid to break the rules.
  2. You are not a man if you're too afraid to use a gun to get your way.
  3. You are not a man if you're too afraid to go to jail.

What you must understand about the "ManTown Man" is that he is a part of those who make the laws. He upholds the law and if required, will enforce the law. He does not fight or use a gun to break the law. He uses his strength and ability to fight for the justice that the law represents.

Going around Fighting everyone and being mean and hateful does not make you strong. Standing up for what's right and serving others does not make you weak. What you believe and your convictions will make all the difference in how you behave and how you treat others. For the "ManTown Man" it is not if you will fight, it is why and how you fight.

IV. Reject the Materialistic Lie

Another lie that is promoted through movies, books, rap songs, and videos is, "Money Makes You, The Man!" When you have money, you can buy diamond rings and gold chains. When you have money, you can buy big houses and fancy cars. When you have money people will flock to you and do whatever you want. You can wear the most expensive clothes and travel the world. Money can cause you to illicit a smile from almost everyone you meet. When you come, crowds will part and allow you to go first.

However, the wise "ManTown Man" knows that money does not make you a man. He knows that what you have in your pockets does not determine who you are in your heart and mind. The "ManTown Man" knows that the crowd follows and respects the money not the man. The crowd will leave the man as soon as he has no money. If you put your trust in money to make you a man, you will lose every time. The "ManTown Man" knows that money is just a tool. It can be used to satisfy "LBT" (Little Boy Thinking) which is centered in fulfilling selfish desires, or, for the "ManTown Man" this tool will not only be used to help self but to benefit and serve others.

The Man Myth Conclusion

It is very important to reject the myths of being a man at the very beginning of your journey. If the wrong roads are known ahead of time you will save yourself so much time and effort. This will open the door to using all of your energy to successfully make progress down the right road. It is very clear that these lies influence our society in a very subtle way.

People encourage you to drink alcohol and say that's what grown folk do. However, when you become addicted people call you everything but a man. Friends think they are doing you a service when they set you up to have casual sex. There is no limit to the teasing experienced concerning having sex. However, if you contract aids or get some girl pregnant these same friends accept no responsibility.

The prisons are filled with so-called tough guys. These are the ones that chose the anti-social role to being a man. But these same tough guys end up being told when and what they can eat and when and where they can sleep. They line up like kindergartners to eat and go to recess. Being mean to people will not make you a man. It will just give people a feeling of justification when you are brought down in pain.

When it comes to clothes, there should be one message that your clothes send to others. That message is the message of modest respect. The message is, I respect myself and my fellow man. We represent who we are by what we say, what we do, and how we look. Let your dress tell the world you are a ManTown Man.

Part 5

"ManTown Men" Stand on Principles

Just like a train uses tracks to keep it going in the right direction the ManTown man uses principles. He uses principles to guide him in the right direction and keep him on track. When faced with hard decisions and difficult situations he has learned to trust wisdom. He trusts the wisdom that can be found in ethical, moral and spiritual principles.

In order to capture some of the power of these principles, I have created some acronyms I call the ManTown Letters. You have already been introduced to (LBT) or little boy thinking. This type of thinking says, "I am the most important thing in the world and others are here to serve me." It also says, "I am free from rules, and I should not face consequences."

ORD - Obey, Respect, and Do the Work

The principle you must be taught to correct this unreal desire is ORD or Obey, Respect, and Do the Work. This principle applies wherever there is responsible leadership. People are required to obey those that have legitimate authority over them. This acronym is one of the golden keys to a successful and productive life. You must know that (ORD) is the principle upon which the whole world functions.

Who Is expected to ORD? The answer to that question is everyone! As American citizens we are expected to obey, respect, and do the work. We are required to obey the laws of the land, respect the constitution and our officials, and show our citizenship by our work and service for our country. Workers or employees are required to obey supervisors and bosses, respect company rules and regulations, and do the work they were hired to do. Teachers are expected to obey the principal, respect school rules and regulations, and do the work required by the schools. Children at home are required to obey their parents or guardians, respect their parents or guardians rules, and do housework and chores.

These are a few examples of a principle that should be learned and practiced by all.

Let's talk about obedience. To have an obedient spirit demonstrates you know how to listen, and you know how to follow instructions. It will cause people to know that they can depend on you and trust you. Getting older does bring more independence, however, it does not erase the need for obedience. No one ever outgrows the need to obey.

What about respect? It is a fact that everyone wants and needs respect. Respect is probably one of the most noble acts we can demonstrate. Respect says that you recognize the value and worth of people. When you give respect, you can rightfully expect to be respected. However, if others don't act respectfully, their actions should not define who you are.

Finally, what does it mean to "Do the work"? This simply means being responsible enough to do the work you have been called to do. It does not matter if it is chores at home or work on a job. Whatever you are responsible for doing, don't procrastinate, be lazy, or negligent. Fulfill the responsibilities.

Those that practice ORD graduate from schools and college, get jobs and promotions, and maintain solid reputations.

If we were living in a perfect world everyone would follow the principle of (ORD), however, we all know this is not a perfect world. There are many that have decided they would rather do the opposite of ORD. This brings us to the next principle we will consider. This principle is the exact opposite of (ORD).

DDD - Don't Obey, Disrespect, Don't Do the Work

If you are wise, you can learn from negative principles as well as positive principles. The negative principles will show you how not to live. We identify this next principle as DDD or Disobey, Disrespect, and Don't do the Work. This represents a rebellious spirit that can exist in anyone and must be intentionally defeated. The following chart explains the definition and consequences that comes from practicing DDD.

The following charts explain the definition and consequences of both principles. These charts show how these principles work in our everyday living.

O   R   D
"Obey - Respect - Do the Work"

What is ORD?

ORD (Obey, Respect, Do the Work) is one of the golden keys to a successful and productive life.

DON'T BE FOOLED! EVERYBODY MUST OBEY! IT'S THE RIGHT THING TO DO!

OBEY	RESPECT	DO THE WORK
[Obedience Is Expected From Everyone.]	[Everybody Wants and Needs Respect.] [Important Values and Things Need To Be Respected.]	[Talk Is Cheap.] [Respect Is Shown Through Action.]

AMERICANS: are required to obey the Constitution.	▶ To respect our Laws & Officials.	▶ To show citizenship by our work and service.
EMPLOYESS: are required to obey Supervisors & Bosses.	▶ To respect Company Rules, Regulations and Officials.	▶ To do the work they were hired to do.
SCHOOL STUDENTS: are required to obey Teachers.	▶ To respect School Rules and Regulations.	▶ To do the work required by the Teacher.
CHILDREN: are required to obey their Parents and Guardians.	▶ To respect your Parents and the House Rules.	▶ To do housework and chores.

The Man Town Letters

D   D   D
"Disobey - Disrespect - Don't Do the Work"

What is DDD?

To be "Disobedient" is to be unruly & rebellious.
To be "Disrespectful" is to be rude, mean, and thoughtless.
To "Don't Do the Work" is to be lazy and useless.

IT IS EASY TO SEE THAT DDD IS THE EXACT OPPOSITE OF ORD:

ORD [Obey, Respect, Do The Work] is one of the golden keys to a good life.
DDD [Disobey, Disrespect, Don't Do The Work] is the formula for misery and a hard life.
DDD Is the key that opens the door to trouble and pain.

"THE CONSEQUENCES OF DDD"

Those that grow up and consistently Disobey the Rules, Disrespect those in authority, and Don't do the Work required of them experience things like:

HOME:	SCHOOL:	JOBS:	MARRIAGE:	SOCIETY:
1. Punishment	1. Failing Grades	1. Demoted	1. Separation	1. Avoided
2. Privileges Taken	2. Retained	2. Fired	2. Divorce	2. Arrested
3. Removal from Home	3. Expelled	3. Fined	3. Arrested	3. Banned
	4. Removed			4. Put In Prison

The Man Town Letters

When I was growing up as one of nine children, experiencing all the pain of poverty and deprivation, I had a cousin my exact age. My cousin was an only child. His family was what I considered rich. When I visited him, he would show me all of his new toys. He would show me all his new outfits and the latest brand of tennis shoes.

I was surprised that my biggest emotion was not jealousy but confusion. Although I had very few material possessions, I had received training in how to respect my elders and do what I was told to do. My cousin had been blessed to be brought up in a home where he could receive whatever his heart desired. However, my cousin was rude and disobedient to his parents and other adults. I kept saying to myself, if I had just some of the things, he had I would be the best-behaved boy in the city.

Without really knowing it, I had been taught "ORD". My cousin, on the other hand, had not been taught "ORD" or he had been taught but rejected the principle. As a result of him not operating on this principle he faced a hard and a painful life, filled with disappointment and punishment.

This was an example of one who chose to live by the "DDD" principle. It is an example of one who chose to DISOBEY, (be rebellious), DISRESPECT, (be mean and thoughtless), and DON'T DO THE WORK, (be laziness and irresponsible). As it has been stated before, "DDD" is the key that opens the door to trouble and pain.

SCSR - Self-Control, Self-Regulation

The next "ManTown" principle is so important that it could determine if a boy ever grows up to make it to "Man Town". This principle is identified by the acronym "SCSR". "SCSR" stands for Self-Control, Self-Regulation.

Let's talk about Self-Control first. In order to understand this principle, I use the operation of a car for an example. When a car is traveling down the highway one of the most important parts of the car is the brakes. If you were traveling 70 miles per hour and you saw a traffic jam up ahead, you would feel the need for brakes. The better your brakes, the less worry you have about your ability to stop yourself. Without brakes you are destined to have an accident. The accident could take your life and perhaps someone else's life as well.

Just like a car needs brakes, you need the power of emotional and psychological brakes. In other words, you need to have the ability to stop yourself. You need to have the ability to say "no" to your desires and passions. You need to be able to say "no" to yourself and mean it. When your mind tells you that you need to stop an action or a thought, that is when you need to have Self-Control. Your passions and desires fuel your emotions and drive your will. But if you don't have Self-Control SC, your emotions will drive you to destruction.

(SC) or Self-Control is not just the ability to stop yourself or quit bad behavior. There is another instrument of a car that SC can be compared to. SC can be compared to the accelerator or what us old folk call the gas petal. Sometimes you may find that you need more get-up and go. There are times you need to pick up the pace. Some tasks, problems, or situations demand more energy and effort if you want to be successful. You must possess the internal power to boost your efforts and increase your physical or mental speed.

To have Self-Control is to stop yourself when engaged in bad behavior, and the ability to increase your efforts to accomplish what is good.

The second part of this principle is SR or Self-Regulation. To understand this principle, we can continue with the car analogy. Self-Regulation can be compared to the steering wheel in a car. It is important to be able to go forward and to stop when needed. However, to reach most destinations you need to be able to turn and change directions when necessary. Sometimes you may find that you're going in the wrong direction. You need not only to have the ability to stop going in the wrong direction, but you also need to be able to turn and go in the right direction. It is not unusual to come to a crossroads where a decision of direction stares you in the face. You will be called upon to go in a totally different direction if you want to succeed. To have SR says you don't have to follow the crowd. Self-Regulation says, I don't have to do what everybody else is doing. SR gives you the power to turn you whole life around. You have the power to go in the direction that is best for you. You are not in the back seat letting peers take you where they want to take you. You have the steering wheel of your life. You have the power to turn your life in the direction you see fit. When you put these two together SC-SR and you mix them with wisdom and knowledge you have a formula for success.

(SCSR) Understanding Desires and Passion

S C S R
"Self- ControlSelf- Regulation"

WHAT IS SELF-CONTROL?

Self-Control is to have the ability within to stop yourself and say no to yourself. It is also the power to keep going when you want to stop.

To have Self-Control will allow a person to determine what he will or will not do.

AN EXAMPLE OF SELF-CONTROL:

- Self-Control is like having brakes on a car.
- Without Self-Control we live out of control.
- Good Intentions cannot substitute for self-control.

WHAT IS SELF-REGULATION?

Self-Regulation is the power to determine your own direction and not have to follow the crowd. It is the ability to make wise decisions for yourself.

To have Self-Regulation will allow a person to know the direction he will or will not go.

AN EXAMPLE OF SELF-REGULATION:

- Self-Regulation is like the steering wheel on a car.
- You have the power to turn left or right.
- Self-Regulation is like the gas pedal on a car.
- You can speed up or slow down.

SELF-CONTROL AND SELF-REGULATION EMPOWERS THE DEVELOPMENT OF GOOD CHARACTER!

The Man Town Letters

You must understand that the biological changes that will take place in every young boy's body will make it extremely difficult to have SCSR. Massive amounts of testosterone and other hormones are being dumped into your system. These hormones create strong natural inclinations and unfamiliar desires. You will be inclined to be active and sometimes aggressive. You will be faced with physical desires and sexual arousal. These feelings are not abnormal. These feelings come with getting older.

However, just because these feelings are normal does not mean that they should be allowed to run wild and out of control. This is the time every boy needs a "Man Town Man" in his life. This is a time that a boy needs someone that understands and can support him through this difficult period.

Just like a baby must learn how to control his natural desire to release and must be potty trained, so must a boy be trained to control his instinctual desires and emotions. To be able to have SCSR over your passions and emotions is no small task. In fact, it will be one of the greatest challenges ever. But if you can learn how to control and regulate yourself, it will be one of the greatest and most beneficial accomplishments of your life.

If you have no father that you can look to for this training, do your best to use this material for support. I also suggest you develop a spiritual faith. We need a power greater than ourselves when we face challenges greater than our own strength. Sometimes you need to call on the wisdom of old to handle the problems of the day. The book of proverbs is a good book to study.

Here are a few things you must learn to control and regulate:

A. You Must Learn to Control Your Temper
  1. You must be trained not to allow your anger to take control of your mind.
  2. You must be trained to slow your reactions down and get all the facts before you assume you are right and what action you should take.
  3. You must be trained to not take matters into your own hands and get yourself in trouble. Protect yourself by using the proper officials to address your offenses.

B. You Must Learn to Control Your Tongue
  1. You must be trained to think before you speak.
  2. You must be trained not to use your tongue as a weapon to hurt and destroy.
  3. You must be trained in how to use your tongue to encourage and build people up.
  4. You must be trained not to lie but to speak truth.

C. You Must Learn How to Wait and Have Patience
  1. You must be trained to endure pain.
  2. You must be trained to sometimes put others before yourself.
  3. You must be trained to patiently work for what you want.
  4. You must be trained to not always see yourself as a victim.

To summarize it all, SCSR says your desires, passions, and emotions must be brought under control and be regulated to be a "ManTown Man".

CAE – Change, Adapt, Evolve

C A E
"Change Adapt Evolve"

WHAT THREE (3) THINGS MUST HAPPEN TO A BOY IN ORDER TO BECOME A "MAN"?
A boy must "Change, Adapt, and Evolve" into something totally different than what he was.

WHAT IS MEANT BY "CHANGE"?
The two words that best describes the process of change from a boy to a man is "Metamorphosis" and "Transformation". A boys Transformation is much like the transformation of the caterpillar to a butterfly.

CATERPILLAR AND THE STAGES OF "CHANGE"	ADAPTIONS	EVOLVE	FROM BOYS TO MEN
1st Stage - Egg 2nd Stage - Egg to Larva 3rd Stage - Larva to Caterpillar 4th Stage - Caterpillar to Cocoon 5th Stage - Cocoon to Butterfly	▸ Lived in the Egg _(Now living in the world)_ ▸ From Stationary to Mobile ▸ From Leaves to Nectar ▸ From Crawling to Flying	To evolve is not only to accept the change but be changed in mind and body. It means to never seek to return to what you use to do or be.	_What Must_ _Change, Adapt, Evolve_ ▸ The boys **body** ▸ The boys **mind** ▸ The boys **purpose** and **goals**.

The Man Town Letters

You must remember that "ManTown" is not a physical location. "ManTown" is an evolved state of mind. Unless the mind reaches a certain understanding about life, love, and living you are not in this wonderful city. Therefore, it is important for you to see and understand how your mind changes and develops from "LBT" to "MTT". Nature gives you a wonderful example of this change. The stages you will see in this example will help you to visualize the changes that must take place in your life if you want to make it to "ManTown".

The key word that must be remembered is "Change". A boy cannot continue to think like a boy and be a man. Change must occur. The two words that best describe the process of change from boy to man are "Transformation" and "Metamorphosis". These words suggest that what you may have started with is not what you will end up with. They suggest that when the process is complete there will be a visible difference.

Nature's example for you is the caterpillar's change to a butterfly.

The 1st stage of the caterpillar's existence is in an egg. This is much like you as a baby were in your mother's stomach. When it comes into the world it is called a larva. It is now able to move around more. However, the only thing on its mind is eating and sleeping. The larva eats the very leaf it lives on only to move to other leaves and do the same. The larva will continue to eat and grow until it becomes a caterpillar. The caterpillar can be a menace to leafy vegetation. It destroys gardens and makes little or no contribution to its environment. It simply crawls on its belly, eats and sleeps. One day the caterpillar crawls to a place where it seals itself inside a cocoon. In this dark, tight, restricted space, the caterpillar goes through a change. It will change in so many ways it will no longer be the same. It will change so much it will no longer be called a caterpillar. When it comes from the cocoon it takes on a whole new purpose in life. It will no longer destroy gardens. It will now bring beauty to fields by pollinating flowers. It will no longer crawl on the ground but with its beautiful colors it will fly through the air. Even the appetite of the caterpillar will change when it comes from the cocoon. Instead of eating bitter leaves it now sips sweet nectar from the flowers.

Once the caterpillar leaves the cocoon it changes and will never be a caterpillar again. It is now a butterfly. It no longer thinks like a caterpillar or does what caterpillars do. It must adapt to its new life an embrace it's evolution. From the time it came into existence, it didn't know it but its mission in life was to "Change, Adapt, and Evolve". Its mission was to CAE.

If you can understand nature's examples of change you will understand how you must CAE. Over time, nature will force your body to change from the body of a little boy to an adult male. Nature needs very little help to cause your body to change. However, unless you are taught and trained in the proper Moral, Ethical, and Spiritual Principles of life, your mind will not automatically change. Your body will change but the way you selfishly think will remain the same.

If you study and concentrate on the things presented to you in this material, it will be like putting your LBT mind in a cocoon of transformation. If you learn these principles to live by, you will never be the same. You will have made the transformation from "Boy" to a "ManTown Man".

Part I - ManTown Men "Know How Life Works"

Almost all cars and trucks today are what we call automatic. What that means is that when you drive the car or truck you don't have to change the gears in the vehicle from 1st gear to 2nd gear to 3rd gear and to 4th gear. The car automatically changes gears for you. However, when I was growing up, cars had stick shifts and they were manual. In order to drive the car, you had to know how to shift the gears for yourself. You had to know how things worked.

When you are operating in "LBT" (Little Boy Thinking) you don't think very much about how the car of life works or what you need to do to make it work. The only thing you're concerned with is having it take you where you want to go. The "LBT" mindset keeps you in automatic. As you get older and hopefully more mature you were meant to move away from automatic to manual. You move away from, the mindset of "I automatically have a house to live in, food to eat, and a bed to sleep on." You move away from, "I automatically have clothes to wear, transportation to ride in, and money to spend." When you move from "LBT" to "MTT" (Man Town Thinking) you move from automatic to manual. With "Man Town Thinking" you realize that it is up to you to learn how life works and how to make it work for you. "ManTown Thinking" tells you the only way you don't get stuck in 1st gear is that you learn to shift to 2nd gear and then to 3rdgear. You understand you are responsible for your own life. You know that you must accept the responsibility for your own decisions.

Before I ever got old enough to drive, I would sit in my father's truck and practice shifting gears. By the time I was old enough to drive I already knew what to do.

Listen very carefully to this point! If you take this advice, it will cause you to see what's going on in your life in a completely different way.

The point is this, the practice of shifting gears in my father's truck was the thing that got me ready to drive when I got my own truck. The practice of disciplining yourself to do the things that need to be done, even when it is hard and you don't want to do it, is getting you ready. Believe it or not, cleaning up your room when you don't feel like it is getting you ready. Cleaning your kitchen and taking out the trash is all training for real life. Doing your homework and turning papers in on time is getting you ready for life. These are the things that are preparing you to be responsible for yourself. These things teach you discipline and self-control. The training for you to be a responsible man starts in your home and at school. Reading your bible and going to worship when you are young helps you to develop values and morals when you are older.

When I was in school, I ran track. Day after day I had to force myself to go to practice. Repeatedly I ran around and around the track. When I became tired, I had to train myself to keep running. But upon my graduation, it all paid off. It paid off because in the process I had become fast enough to get a scholarship in track that paid for me to attend college. I was able to receive thousands of dollars because I had trained myself to do what I didn't feel like doing.

You may think that obeying your parents, doing your chores, and studying in school is boring and dumb. However, if you only knew how it is preparing and training you to be ready to get the best out of life, you would feel different about doing it.

The fact is it was never meant for someone to take care of you forever. If you are not severely sick physically or psychologically at some point you were meant to take care of yourself. You need to start now learning how to care for yourself. This will also prepare you to care for others that may need your help. However, you can't help others when you can't even help yourself. Before you become a "Life Guard" that helps those who can't swim you must first learn to swim yourself.

What's my point? Change the way you see life! Don't see life like a spoiled, selfish, permanent baby boy. Look at life and your responsibilities as the training ground to one day be a man.

Part II - ManTown Men "Know How Life Works"

Someone has said almost everything is created twice. The first creation is in the mind and the second creation is created in the physical world. If this is true, and I truly believe that it is, then the things created in the mind become extremely important. The mind is the playground of a person's imagination. In your mind you can think of the wildest things. The mind can be the laboratory for the greatest inventions and the deadliest schemes. The mind can be the home of the most honorable intentions and the birthplace of the evilest plans.

Here is where the fun begins. If you have ever seen a picture of a cowboy trying to ride and tame a wild horse then that is a perfect example of what you must do to your mind. If you don't tame or learn to control your mind, your mind will run wild. We all know that wild horses love to run wild with other wild horses. A good example of this can be seen in street gangs and gangsters in city mobs. The problem with the wild mind is that there are no rules that it respects. The wild mind is almost always centered on self. The wild mind is not reliable, dependable, or responsible. The focus on the wild mind is generally not on others but rather pleasure, excitement, power, and privilege.

SPF - Seed, Plant, Fruit

The way the mind works is it produces thoughts. I will call these thoughts seeds. Just like a seed has within it the power to produce so does the mind have within it the power to produce. This brings me to the "ManTown" principle of "SPF". This stands for (Seed, Plant, Fruit). To understand the concept of "SPF" is to understand how all things work. As was stated before, the mind produces thoughts. These thoughts are like seeds. The "P" represents the planting of the seed. For our analogy, the planting of the seed is the action taken because of the thought. So, the seed is the thought and the action taken because of the thought is the plant. The "F" or Fruit is the consequences that result from the actions taken because of the thought. If every thought is a seed then bad thoughts will promote bad actions which will result in bad consequences. Good seeds or thoughts will promote good actions which most of the time lead to good consequences.

I say most of the time because doing right is always good, but it can sometimes be costly and painful. However, "ManTown Men" do what is right because of the morals they have developed and are willing to face the pain. "ManTown Men" stand up for what they believe in, and they believe in doing right.

The mind takes in information from the outside to come up with thoughts on the inside. In other words, the mind uses the senses. It receives information from the eyes, the sounds from the ears, taste from the tongue, and sensations from touch. The senses can release chemicals and hormones in our bodies. These chemicals and hormones can influence the mind to think certain thoughts. For example, tasting certain drugs and alcohol can cause you to think that you can do things you cannot do. When intoxicated with alcohol you may think you can drive a car. The seed is the thought, driving the car is the plant, and the consequences could be death for you, others, or both. If you are going to control your thoughts, you will have to protect your mind. You protect your mind by not allowing your senses to be exposed to everything. For example, when your eyes are exposed to porn, and your ears hear sexual lyrics and sounds it releases chemicals in your body. These chemicals affect your mind and cause you to think certain sexual thoughts. Without the sensual stimulation you would never have thought the thoughts. These thoughts may lead to certain acts. The consequences of these acts can lead to unwanted pregnancies, rape, cheating, and negatively altered lives. What does it mean to protect your mind? One way to protect your mind is to restrict your senses. You must be careful about what you allow your eyes to see, what you permit your ears to hear, what you allow your mouth to taste, and your hands to touch. You must remember, everything starts with the thought. Let your mind sow good seed or good thoughts. Then you will want to do good things which will result in worthy consequences. "SPF" is the way life works.

Part 6

How Boys Turn Into Men

Willie B. Williams

Narcissistic Personality Disorder

Children come into this world with great possibilities. In this study we have focused our attention on the development of boys to men. When a baby boy is born the hope of a joyful, fulfilling journey begins. However, certain things early in the life of a boy can often times predict just how successful that journey will be. According to the Diagnostic Statistical Manual of Mental Disorders or DSM-5 published by the American Psychiatric Association, there is a condition disproportionate to males. This condition affects more males than females. The condition we are speaking of is referred to as "NPD" or The Narcissistic Personality Disorder. The Narcissistic Personality Disorder is defined by the DSM -5 as "an enduring pattern of inner experience and behavior that deviates markedly from the individuals culture, is pervasive and inflexible, has an onset in adolescence or early adulthood, is stable over time, and leads to distress or impairment".

From this definition we learn that this disorder shows its first signs in childhood or adolescence. Once this disorder is allowed to develop it is said to be pervasive. This means that it will affect all areas of an individual's life. It is inflexible, which means that it is rigid and hard to change. It is said to be stable over time. This means that this condition is lasting, enduring, and can be permanently entrenched in a person's personality. Finally, this disorder sets forth a prediction that those that have this disorder will end up distressed and impaired or damaged psychologically.

In the DSM -4 it was claimed that up to 75% of those diagnosed with this disorder were male. The Narcissistic Personality Disorder falls into what is psychologically considered Cluster B disorders. This Cluster of disorders also includes antisocial behavior such as the sociopath and the psychopath. The DSM -5 states, "antisocial personality disorder is much more common in males than in females."

There are three reasons, if you are a young male, to start working on yourself now if you don't want to fall into this disorder. The first reason is that the majority of those identified with these antisocial disorders are male. The second reason is that this disorder begins to develop in childhood or adolescence. Finally, if this disorder is not addressed early, it may become permanent, bringing you distress and possibly destroying your life and the lives of others.

There is no medication that can be taken to cure this disorder. It is believed by some that this condition is brought on more by environmental factors than inheritance. In other words, how you are raised greatly determines if you contract this disorder.

As a young boy, the way to best avoid these personality disorders is to embrace moral, ethical, and spiritual principles.

The Core

A core is defined as that part of something that is central to its existence or character. The core of a person is their fundamental belief system. Your core is what you believe about life and what you value the most. The narcissistic personality values self the most. The narcissistic personality is totally connected to "LBT" or little boy thinking. The narcissistic personality will lie, cheat, steal, manipulate, and bully to satisfy self at the expense of everyone else. The opposite of this core, life view, or value system is a core value system that embraces the time-tested moral, ethical, and spiritual beliefs such as:

- Honesty is the best policy.
- Do unto others as you would have them do to you.
- You must work for what you want.
- You will reap what you sow.
- What is done in the dark will one day come to the light.

The Filter

If these types of principles are in your core personality, then life situations will be filtered through these values. If you have these values, it will change the questions you ask yourself in certain situations. Instead of first asking yourself what do I want, you will ask yourself what do others need? Your problems will be filtered through your world view, your principles and your value system before you decide or respond in an action. Your core values will tell you how to interpret both the good and the bad. Your core values will tell you what you should and should not do. These core values are more in line with "ManTown Thinking".

Wet Cement

If you have seen wet cement being poured from a cement truck, you will notice that it takes the shape of whatever it is poured into. If it is wet its shape can be changed and molded. However, overtime it begins to harden. Once the cement hardens into whatever form it was poured into it is almost impossible to change it. This is the same process that can be seen in the development of your character. The things you do on a regular basis, over time, become part of how you see yourself. If you never clean up your room or wash the dishes you grow to feel that cleaning up after you is someone else's job. If you practice getting your way no matter how it hurts others, you will begin to feel that you are entitled to get what you want, and others are not. If, when you get angry, you lose control and throw a fit of rage and break things that will be how you will learn to handle frustration.

This is why you must work hard now before your bad habits, addictions, and disorders become hardened and permanent. If a person is alive, it is never too late to change. But it is much easier to change a thought than it is to change a habit. Events, relationships, and all types of situations will be filtered through your core values. Make sure you have "ManTown" values before your core becomes too hard to change.

Part 7

ManTown Men Know How to Communicate

The Art of Communication

Understanding the Art of Communication is one of the most important lessons you can learn. I call it art because it is a skill that is not only necessary and beneficial, but it can also be beautiful. Good communication can ease tension, promote unity, and provide clarity. Fewer mistakes and misunderstandings happen when good communication exists. Good communication prevents people from being verbally abused, disrespected, or misrepresented. Where there is verbal abuse and disrespect, relationships are easily destroyed.

Why is Communication Important?

The reason communication is so important is because it is the basis of all relationships. It is the heart of civilization. Not only that, but communication is also one of our greatest human needs, and one of the greatest tools for cooperation. Poor cooperation or a lack of communication causes conflicts and misunderstandings. It results in arguments, violence, angry outburst, shutting down, walking away, and giving up. One of the top reasons for divorce is due to communication problems. According to research published in the journal of Divorce and Remarriage, the two most common reasons divorcing parents cited as their motivation for divorce were "growing apart" (55%) and not being able to talk together" (53%). According to one study 67.5% of marriages ended because of bad or a lack of communication.

What is Communication?

Communication can be defined as the process by which information is exchanged between individuals. It is exchanged through a common system of symbols, signs, and behavior. It must be understood that communication is binary and never mono in nature. What that means is that there are always two disciplines that must take place in order for there to be communication. The process of communication always includes both sending and receiving and never just sending. In other words, if the message you sent was not received, you have not communicated. However, when I say a message received, I am not saying that the message must be agreed to, only that it was understood as the sender gave it.

The element of understanding in communication is essential. Understanding is one of the foremost goals of communication. When you talk, you want to be understood, and when others talk to you, they long for you to understand. Understanding, in communication is equivalent to physical sight. Just as the eyes allow us to see physically, we use our mind to see mentally. When someone is communicating, if I don't understand then I can't see. If I can't understand or see then I can't obey nor be persuaded to change my mind.

How Does Communication Work?

There are three major elements involved in the process of communication:

- The first element is the "Declaration" or the message.
- The second element is the "Reception" or receiving the message.
- The third element is the Transformation" or the impact of the message.

We make our declarations through our message. Communication always begins with the message. However, the message sent does not have to be words. Babies communicate their needs by crying or whining. There are several ways messages are sent in an effort to communicate. Messages are sent through words, body language, voice inflections, rhythm of speech, pitch, energy, and even cooperation. Many messages are given even when no words have been spoken. People tend to believe body language and non-verbal queues even more than they believe what a person may say. In fact, words carry the lease value in the messages sent. If your body language says you are angry, and your words say you are not angry most people will tend to believe your body language.

The reception of the message is an internal process. The message is interpreted in the mind. The acknowledgment of the reception can be demonstrated through words and action. If the message called for an action and the action was not done, most of the time the sender will feel that his message was not received. There was no impact or transformation that would demonstrate the message was understood.

Respect In Communication

In society today the element of respect in communication has to a great degree been abandoned. The boundaries in the way we communicate in society today have been erased. If you are ever going to be an effective communicator you must understand and accept the role that respect plays in your ability to communicate effectively. There are those that through relationship, position, rank, or service deserve certain acknowledgment. The way you communicate with them shows that you respect or disrespect them. What I mean is that there should be a difference between the way you speak to your parents and the way you speak to your little friends down the street. There should be a difference between the way you talk to your teacher or your principal and the way you talk to your classmates. There should be a difference between the way a husband or wife speaks to one another and the way they talk to the kids.

Many wives refuse to hear what their husbands says because she says, "you talk to me as if I am a child". The difference she is looking for can only be found if the husband understands one thing. He must understand that as a wife she deserves a certain level of respect. His respect for her must affect the way that he communicates with her. He cannot just say anything to her. In his respect he must be able to restrain himself and conduct himself in a way that demonstrates his respect. This respect will affect his speech and communication.

The respect that is due to a husband and wife creates boundaries in speech and behavior between the two of them. Responsible parents have the right and duty to demand that children obey their word. Respect and understanding the roles in marriage will prevent the husband or the wife from ordering each other to do anything. Husband and wives don't demand each other, they make requests.

When I was growing up, we as children were taught to say, "yes sir" and "no sir", or "yes ma'am" and "no ma'am" to those who had earned the positional respect of being an adult. However, there are some adults who do not want this type of respect because they do not want to acknowledge their age. They literally teach children not to see them as older. They teach children to see them as the same in age and maturity. They don't want to be seen as older but rather just one of the gang. This is unfortunate because children that need to learn how to respect those that are older are taught not to respect. As you move from boy to man, you must be willing to accept the responsibility that comes with age. There is an expected maturity that even society expects to come with age. That is where the whole idea of the "Chaperone" comes from. Children are to be chaperoned by adults because they are expected to be more responsible and mature. If an adult is in the presence of youth, the adult is often held responsible for what the youth are allowed to do. Adults should be respected. But it must be understood that with respect comes responsibility. A boy should show respect to all but especially to those that are over him. The respect you show will be more about who you are and your character than anything else. Although these respected boundaries are quickly disappearing, at least at school, students are still instructed to refer to their teachers as Ms. Johnson or Mr. Matthews instead of Susie and Billy.

Listening In Communication

The reason we started this study of communication with the element of respect is because respect is clearly connected with good listening. People tend to not listen to those they do not respect. You must develop a genuine sense of respect for all mankind. You must understand that a basic human need is to express thoughts and feelings and to be understood. Just as you want to be heard and understood, grant this privilege to others.

The listening that comes through the filter of respect is more focused on what is being said than on making a quick reply. The purpose for listening is to truly hear and understand. Respecting a person does not mean that you automatically agree with what the person may present. However, it does mean that you have the skill to put your thoughts and feelings on hold long enough to genuinely hear and understand what the other person is saying.

Meaningful listening will not only include the words but the tone and the body language. Meaningful listening will include understanding the situation and circumstances surrounding the words being spoken. For instance, if a person just got fired from their job and comes home in a bad mood, their words and actions may not be what they should be. A good listener will consider the situation and may even hear the fact that they are speaking from their pain. A good listener may even ask the person about their day and give them an opportunity to talk about what's really on their mind. To truly listen you need empathy. Empathy is the ability to understand and share the feelings of another person. This brings us to the mechanics of communication.

The Mechanics of Communication

A psychologist by the name of Edward Thorndike proposed the "Stimulus – Response Theory." A stimulus is anything that gets your attention, and a response is how you react to what got your attention.

When someone is speaking to you it should get your attention. If you have developed respect for people, you will not practice ignoring someone when they are talking to you. When someone is speaking to you, you will give them your attention. This will be your stimulus. The attention you give is actually one of the ways respect for the speaker is shown. However, how you respond is critical. In several situations many people automatically respond to something said or done to them without thinking. However, good communication calls for a few steps to take place between the stimulus and the response. The following is a good formula for effective communication.

- Stimulus
- Consideration
- Investigation
- Determination
- Response

Consideration

We have already identified the stimulus as someone or something that gets your attention. The next thing that should take place is to consider the surrounding situation and circumstances. I sometimes give the example of a person being tackled on a football field while playing football verses being tackled on a public street. Although the pain of being tackled is the same and the person may be the same, to consider the situation will add to the appropriateness of the response. Being tackled on a football field should influence how you feel about being tackled. You may not like it, but it is not the same as being tackled on a public street and should be thought of differently. (It is appropriate to be tackled on a football field while playing football. Therefore, this is not a problem. It is not appropriate to tackle someone on the street. Therefore, this may be a problem.) In communication, when someone offends you, instead of immediately responding, consider the surrounding situation.

Investigation

The next thing that should be done is to investigate. Probe for more information. If something happened that you didn't like, you already know how you feel and what you think caused it to happen. However, there may be some facts that would cause you to feel a different way if you took the time to investigate. Your mother tells you that you won't be able to go to the football game tonight. You don't feel that it is right for her to tell you that you can't go. You first want to respond in anger but instead you investigate and find out there has been an accident and your sister is in the hospital. Those new facts change everything.

Now that you have these new facts it's even harder for you to be upset about the game. Before you respond, get the facts and don't just assume. Many hurt feelings and bad decisions have been caused by people who respond before they get the truth. Try to understand the other person's side before you close the case and respond. In order to gain a good understanding, you may have to ask questions for clarification. You may have to restate what was said to make sure you understood correctly. You can't respond correctly if you don't have the truth.

You received the stimulus; you have made your considerations and conducted your investigation. It is now time for you to make your determination.

Determination

The proper determination has taken into consideration all of the facts known and unknown. One of the most dangerous practices used by so many is the lazy practice of deciding or reaching a conclusion based on assumptions that may or may not be true. We then treat these guesses as if they were proven truth. Determinations are what we come to believe. What we believe affects how we feel and what we do. This is why it is so important that you take the time to get knowledge, asks questions, and consider the facts before you decide what you think is true or false.

Response

The one thing that you need more than anything else for this step is wisdom. You must determine which response is the proper response. You must ask yourself," Which response is the correct response." "Which response fits my "Man-Town" character." "Which response will protect me from getting myself in unnecessary trouble. "Remember, you can say the right thing in the wrong way. Your determination of how you will respond should represent the kind of person you know yourself to be. How you respond will literally tell people who you are no matter what you say. In other words, don't let your response cause you to act out of character.

I know that this seems like a lot of work for just a regular conversation. Although it may seem like a long process, with practice, it can be done very quickly. It will cause you to think before you speak. It will cause you to make less mistakes. It will allow you to stay true to your convictions and beliefs. It will also allow you to enjoy rich communication avoiding misunderstandings, arguments, and hurt feelings.

Conclusion

If you as a male accept your biological assignment to be a man, there is only one place for you to go. That one place to go is "ManTown". The road to "Man-Town is not an easy road to travel. Remember, the miles to "ManTown are not physical miles. It is a mental journey traveled over a period of years. As the physical body must go through its development so does the mind have to go through its development. However, you will need help to make it to "ManTown". You were never meant to travel there all on your own. God through nature provided each boy with a biological male father whose job it was to see that their sons make it from boyhood to manhood.

There are countless reasons why these fathers don't do their intended jobs. Sometimes these fathers have good reasons for not being present to do their duty. In some cases, there is sickness and even death. In some cases, they may be soldiers in the armed services. However, there are countless fathers who do not take their role seriously. They refuse to put the time in to teach and train their boys so that they grow up to be dependable, responsible, spiritual men.

It is the responsibility of the father to show the son what it feels like to be loved so that he will be able to give love. It is the job of the father to be truthful so that the son will learn to be honest. It is the duty of the father to love and take care of the children and the mother of the children so that their son would know to love his children and take care of his wife.

The father is assigned the task of introducing his son to the moral, ethical, and spiritual principles of life. The father is to model and train their son in the ways of wisdom. He is to demonstrate the art of living with integrity and demonstrate responsibility.

The boys that don't receive this training are forced to do the best they can. They must observe and learn from the mistakes of others. They must find help wherever they can. So many boys never make it to "ManTown" because they had no man. It is my hope that this material will be of some benefit to countless boys so that they can find the help they need to enter the gates of this glorious place we call "ManTown".

References

American Psychiatric Association. (2000). *Personality Disorders*. In Diagnostic and statistical manual of mental disorders (4th ed.) Narcissistic Personality Disorder. (pg. 717)

American Psychiatric Association. (2022). *Personality Disorders*. In Diagnostic and statistical manual of mental disorders (5th ed.) Narcissistic Personality Disorder. (pg. 669-672)

Biddulph, S. (1998). *Raising boys*. Celestial Arts.

Bly, R. (2004). *Iron John: A Book About Men*. Da Capo Press. (28-44)

Brecheen, C. & Faulkner, P. (1994). *What Every Family Needs: Whatever Happened To Mom, Dad & The Kids*. Gospel Advocate Company.

Brizendine, L. (M.D.). (2010) *The Male Brain*. Harmony.

Campbell, K. W. (Ph.D.). & Crist, C. (2020). *The new science of narcissism*. Sounds True.

Cherry, D.L. (Dr.). (2004). *Child Proofing your marriage: Keeping your marriage a priority during the parenting years*. Life Journey.

Dobson, J. (Dr.). (2002) *Dr. James Dobson's Bringing Up Boys*. Focus on the Family. (9-33)

Eifert, G. (Ph.D.). & McKay. M. (Ph.D.). & Forsyth, J. (Ph.D.). (2006). *Act on life not on anger: The new acceptance & commitment therapy guide to problem anger*. New Harbinger Publications, Inc.

Golomb, E. (Ph.D.). (1992). *Trapped in the Mirror: Adult children of narcissists in their struggle for self*. Quill Williams Morro. (11-23)

Hawkins, A.J. & Willoughby, B.J. & Doherty. W.J. (2012). *Reasons for divorce and marital recognition.* Journal of Divorce & Remarriage. (Vol. 53, No.6)

Jantz. G. (PH.D.) . & Gurian, M. (2013). *Raising boys by design: What the bible and brain science reveals about what your son needs to thrive.* Waterbrook Press.

Liversay, J. USA Today. March 7, 2023.

Maxwell, J.C. (2023) *The 16 undeniable laws of communication: Apply them and make the most of your message.* Maxwell Leadership.

Morley, P. (2013). *How God makes men: Ten epic stories. Ten proven principles. One huge promise for your life.* Multnomah Books. (6-17)

Mueller, C. USA Today, J. December 6, 2022.

Smalley, G. & Tent, J. (Ph.D.). (1992). *The Hidden Value of a Man: The incredible impact of a man on his family.* Focus On The Family Publishing.

The National Center for Health Statistics (2021)

The National Statistics Domestic Violence Fact Sheet

The Social Science & Medicine Vol 146 Dec.2015, pg. 249-256.

USA Census Bureau. (2022). *Living arrangements of children under 18 years old to present.* Washington, D.C.: US Census Bureau

Weinstein, Bruce Ph.D., *Life Principles: Feeling Good by Doing Good*

Milton Keynes UK
Ingram Content Group UK Ltd.
UKHW052305280324
440326UK00001B/14